UNRECEPTIVE

Tom Stanfill

UNRECEPTIVE

A BETTER WAY TO SELL, LEAD, AND INFLUENCE

HARPERCOLLINS
LEADERSHIP

An Imprint of HarperCollins

Published by HarperCollins Leadership, an imprint of HarperCollins Focus LLC.

Any internet addresses, phone numbers, or company or product information printed in this book are offered as a resource and are not intended in any way to be or to imply an endorsement by HarperCollins Leadership, nor does HarperCollins Leadership vouch for the existence, content, or services of these sites, phone numbers, companies, or products beyond the life of this book.

ISBN 978-1-4002-2581-1 (eBook)

ISBN 978-1-4002-2580-4 (HC)

Library of Congress Control Number: 2021942226

Printed in Italy

21 22 23 24 25 GV   10 9 8 7 6 5 4 3 2 1

To Mom and Dad.
The genesis of this book started with you.
You taught me the most important truths in life
and the source of all truth.

For Claire and my family.

CONTENTS

PART IV:
THE FOURTH BARRIER—Changing Their Beliefs

PART V:
THE FIFTH BARRIER—TAKING ACTION

INTRODUCTION

In the early 1990s, I had a simple idea that would change the trajectory of my career forever. At the time, I was working as a sales representative and observed that most salespeople spend the majority of their time doing what they enjoy least: searching for people to call. Now, this was the '90s. There was no email, we were still enamored with fax machines, and flip phones were still hot! As a seller, I understood my job was research and rejection: finding people to call and being told "no, thanks" with a few yeses sprinkled in here and there. Selling, in other words, was 95 percent rejection.

Since most of my peers had the same pain points as me, I started a company to remove the grueling tasks of lead generation and appointment setting. Our company made the calls and generated leads, and the sellers just had to sell. Soon, I was overseeing a hundred bright-eyed, college-aged sales reps who were doing the "dirty work" of making thousands of calls per month, and that's when I had an insight: people weren't rejecting a product or service when they said no to a meeting; they were rejecting a sales call.

Now, these leads were vetted prospects who needed a solution to a recognized problem, but regardless of how compelling the offer was, most people quickly ended the call. Logic and truth just didn't seem to matter. In addition to running a large sales force, I was also married with four kids under the age of thirteen and noticed a similar pattern at home. When a rational argument was presented (by me, of course), I rarely heard, "Oh, good point, Dad, I guess I was wrong . . ." or "You're right, so right, my love. Let's talk about the budget this weekend and how I can cut back on my trips to TJ Maxx." I also noticed heated conversations in culture around race, religion, and politics. No matter where I looked—whether at home, at work, or at a party—no one seemed to be influencing anyone anymore. There had to be a better way.

In my mind, communication was supposed to work like a courtroom: you made your argument, someone reviewed the facts, and civilized rules governed the debate. After hearing all the evidence, there would be a ruling, and all parties would agree on who "won" the debate, shaking hands and moving on. I soon realized the rules that govern a courtroom don't apply to the world I lived in.

Whether it was a pharmaceutical rep talking to a physician about a lifesaving drug or a real estate agent trying to explain the value of a home, good people were far too often closed to the truth. The traditional approach to influence, even with the best argument, often backfired, leading to a less-than-ideal outcome.

To make matters worse, the positions never changed. In fact, people often became *more* entrenched in their original position after an argument. There was something fundamentally broken about the way we were communicating at home, with our friends, and at work. Over the most important topics, people were drawing battle lines that often left relationships fractured and no one persuaded of anything. I wanted to know why.

How do you get prospects to see that you can help them solve a problem that would radically improve their business?

How can you get teenagers to see that drinking and driving could kill them?

How do you help someone see they are racist or persuade an addict to get treatment or have a productive conversation with your spouse about money?

Answering these questions became my passion. I started searching out the brightest minds in behavioral psychology, looking for the answers to why emotions, not truth, seemed to drive the most important conversations. We developed a new approach and began putting it into practice, eventually building a training program based on the principles discovered. It was around this time that BlueCross contacted us. To vet the quality of our services, they wanted to see how we trained our sellers. They quickly embraced our innovative approach to selling and prospecting and hired us to not only generate leads—even with our handmade posters and poorly designed training books—but to train their entire sales force. When I saw these theories of influence and communication were winning over even the most unreceptive customers and prospects, I sold the lead-gen company and started a training company.

At ASLAN, an international sales training company I started with a close friend and head of training at our previous firm, we are now in our twenty-sixth year of teaching sellers and leaders what we've learned about converting the Unreceptive. So much has changed since we started, but a lot has stayed the same. In some ways, people are more closed than ever: we all are increasingly connected to our "tribe" of people who think as we do and reinforce our biases while being isolated from those who might disagree with us. Social media and curated news feeds deliver information that aligns with our strongly held beliefs, and many of us are too overwhelmed to even consider an alternative to what we think is true.

This book is a culmination of twenty-five years of research and field testing about what it takes to break through the walls that divide us and change those strongly held beliefs. Whether it's about social change, the best way to solve business problems, or convincing your daughter to break up with a guy who is no good for her, the traditional approach to communicating fails us when attempting to persuade someone who is unreceptive.

What follows is the antidote.

UNRECEPTIVE

ONE

Traditional Selling Doesn't Work

When someone is emotionally closed, the more you try to persuade
them, the more closed they become. To influence, shift your focus from
selling to creating receptivity.

You got the meeting. You had the right people in the room. You even nailed your presentation. But for no logical reason, a less-qualified competitor was selected for the project. And from the very moment you stepped into the room, you knew it. You could tell by the body language of the decision makers, by subtle shifts in their expressions and how they moved in their chairs: things were not going well. Their arms were folded, a glazed look filled their eyes. They just weren't digging you. And the meeting ended with a conciliatory: "Thanks for the time, great stuff. We'll look it over." And, of course, all you hear next is . . . crickets.

You've worked with a customer for years. The customer has purchased a few products from you but for years now has been closed to other solutions you offer that are clearly superior to the competition. You know if you "go there," it won't go well. You've sent several emails, left your best voice mail, and even though you know the customer needs your solution, you can't get a meeting despite your best efforts.

You're meeting with a team member who shuts down any attempt at helpful feedback even though the person would sorely benefit from it. Your sixteen-year-old daughter is dating a senior with a less-than-stellar reputation, and you want to warn her of potential problems; but there is no hope of delivering the message without a fight. You're talking politics with a friend, debating the afterlife with a relative, or have an opinion on the latest social justice fad. And it is now that you realize you are no longer debating ideas; emotions are in the driver's seat. The conversation is over; the conflict has begun.

Influencing people, when they are emotionally closed, is difficult if not nearly impossible. I've spent the last thirty years dedicated to solving the most difficult riddle in selling, which is to help people make better decisions. After spending thousands of hours studying how the brain works, meeting with PhDs in behavioral psychology about what drives decision-making, and observing thousands of sales interactions, I've learned that not only do our instincts lead us down the wrong path, but everything we've learned about selling sabotages our ability to convert the Unreceptive.

The percentage of decision makers who are receptive to meeting or embracing a new solution is very small. If the customer is emotionally closed, your value proposition, insights, and solution don't matter. Neuroscientists have proven that when emotions elevate, the logical side of the brain shuts off. The traditional approach just doesn't work when dealing with the Unreceptive, which explains why the percentage of sellers who achieve quota has declined for five years in a row in the most robust economy in history. To convert the disinterested, sellers must develop a new mindset and skill set. If they do, they can see engagement rates increase by up to 800 percent and double the average close rate—as my colleagues and I have observed for years.

What I'm about to share has been street-tested for decades. Not only have I practiced these principles and strategies for more than thirty years as a seller, leader, spouse, and parent; my company has also trained and coached more than a hundred thousand sellers in thirty-five countries on these concepts. This way of selling is a radically different approach to sales, one we've proved over and over again. My personal passion is to make these truths available to everyone—yes, to the sales rep who's struggling to make that monthly commission but also to the teachers and parents and friends who sincerely want to persuade someone they love to change their mind for the better.

A BETTER WAY TO PERSUADE

When we started a sales training company, we had no idea it would go global. My title says I run the company, but really I do two things: sell and focus on making it easier for others to sell.

Sales is a funny game in which you either get the gold medal or nothing at all. No one gets into this field because they want to fail, me included, but for most, it's very difficult to hit your number. A high percentage of salespeople cannot convert the Unreceptive, those who are emotionally closed to meeting or hearing about a new solution. Most salespeople simply assume this is just how it is.

You take the losses with the wins (and there are a lot more losses). But when only a small fraction of customers is willing to engage or even after getting a meeting you still lose to a substandard competitor, it can be frustrating. But what if you didn't have to hound your prospects or jump through a million hoops to get the deal?

What if there was another way?

For three decades, I have tried to answer one important question: What can we do to make selling more effective and more enjoyable? What if the number of people who responded to your cold emails and phone calls could not only double but triple? What if clients invited you into the conversation with competitors, asking you to sit at the table when they weren't sure what to do? What if they responded to your questions with the unvarnished truth and didn't treat you like an adversary but an ally? This sales fantasy is attainable, but for most of us it requires a counterintuitive approach, like learning to trust your GPS even when it seems to be taking you in the wrong direction.

For most of us, this experience can feel like a tug-of-war between you and your potential customers. You approach them, and their defenses go up. Sensing this resistance, you offer your best "objection crusher," and they feel they're being talked into something, so they start making excuses. You counter those excuses with a little pressure to explain what's really holding them back, but they only get more defensive. And so it goes, back and forth, each tug prompting an equal and reciprocal tug.

We have been taught the secret to successful sales is to win—that is, to tug harder. It's not. When you change the game and help them see you are actually on their side, that you want them to win no matter what, you earn their trust. Our goal as sellers is not to "beat" our customers in a struggle for control. Our goal is to influence because, when we become better influencers, we become better sellers.

Don't you want to get rid of that constant feeling of groveling for attention and having to force your way into meetings? Wouldn't it be great if clients came to you and asked what you thought they should do? Don't you wish you could focus more on figuring out the best way to solve their problems instead of just fighting to get their attention?

You can—if you start thinking like a farmer.

SEED MENTALITY: FINDING FERTILE SOIL

His neck was worn like a saddle. He had the hands of a man who had worked hard all his life, and when he introduced himself, I felt like I was meeting John Wayne. I liked him instantly. Henry Owen was in his mid-sixties, a fourth-generation farmer who had managed over a thousand acres in Southern California just north of Los Angeles. His most profitable client was Sunkist, and he was, as my dad would say, the backbone of America.

We met while playing golf in Kauai. I was there celebrating my thirty-fifth wedding anniversary and decided to check out the course. Getting partnered with Henry, who owned a time-share nearby, was one of the highlights of my trip. I was curious about a world so foreign to mine. Living off the land, depending on the elements to survive, he was the mysterious source of food that wound up on my table every night, and I wanted to get to know the man who lived such a life.

Somewhere around the eighth hole, I asked Henry what the most important aspect of producing a crop. Was it how you irrigated the fields? Maybe a genetically altered seed that allowed a farmer to grow oranges in half the time? He didn't blink before answering: "If the soil ain't fertile, it just don't matter." There are certain seeds, he explained, that can lead to better fruit, but the most important element is the soil. If it's not good soil, it doesn't matter how good the seed is; you're never going to turn a good harvest. Without realizing it, Henry had captured what so many of us in sales overlook. Almost everything we've learned about selling sabotages our chances of converting the disinterested, because we've overlooked the preparation of the soil.

We sellers tend to have a seed mentality, and in the words of Henry, that "just don't work."

In sales, we are taught to make plausible arguments for why our solution benefits the customer, but we are rarely if ever taught to focus on the customer's level of openness. Focusing on the message first is a perspective that may be killing your ability to find and close deals. Why?

Because a customer's willingness to listen is more important than your ability to communicate. And a willingness to listen, in this day and age, is in steep decline. I call this willingness to listen "receptivity." When someone is emotionally open to you, they are far more willing to listen to what you have to say and buy what you're selling. When someone is emotionally closed, however, the more you try to persuade, the more closed they become. Therefore, you need to shift from selling to focusing on creating receptivity.

Although most prospects are typically closed to sellers, there are simple ways to change that, to help them become more receptive, and it can happen quickly if you know what you're doing.

Cultivating this ability and showing you how to help emotionally "closed" people open up will be the focus of this book.

INFORMATION AND ISOLATION

In the last fifty years, media consumption has increased to almost ten hours per day per person. We are barraged with over five thousand daily messages across hundreds of channels to choose from.

For salespeople, the problem is twofold. First, the availability of information reduces the need for a rep as the primary educator of solutions (that is, "Why do I need to talk with you if I can just google it?"). Second, your email or phone call is getting buried. The net effect is you're more unwanted than ever, which is why the response rate to prospecting emails is below 3 percent and cold calls lead to an appointment only 0.3 percent of the time. It's why many have declared cold-calling to be dead.

What's disheartening is that the most popular solution to overcome this daily overexposure to media is to send more messages. The Keller Research Center at Baylor University conducted a widely publicized study that produced the stats above and concluded: "Bottom-line, increasing engagement [that is, sending more messages] will help break through the clutter of not only the hundreds of ad exposures per day, but the thousands of ads and brand exposures." Really? The greater the resistance in your customer, the more you should increase the frequency of your message? Isn't that what we've *been* doing? This might be a viable approach for the marketing department, but it's killing sales. Nonetheless, this is the only advice we've been offered: Work harder, send more messages, make more calls. Tug harder. The typical result? Increased resistance. Those numbers above haven't changed for decades, and that's because those efforts are missing the point. The number of times you attempt to share your message doesn't matter if the recipient has the consistency of dried concrete. You've got to prepare the soil. You have to understand how to gauge their receptivity.

In addition, we are increasingly isolated from those who think differently from the way we do. Social media algorithms reward us for likes and follows with more content that reinforces what we already believe, creating an echo chamber of information. During the 2004 presidential campaign, a researcher named Drew Westen took MRI photos of the brains of staunch supporters of both George W. Bush and John Kerry. The neuroimaging revealed that when participants were shown their favorite political candidates contradicting themselves, the part of the brain that controls reasoning shut down while the emotional part of the brain lit up. Not only did the reasoning part go dormant, the part of the brain that rewarded selective behavior was engaged.

In Westen's words, "Essentially, it appears as if partisans twirl the cognitive kaleidoscope until they get the conclusions they want, and then they get massively reinforced for it, with the elimination of negative emotional states and activation of positive ones." In simple terms, when people are faced with an idea or subject they have a strong bias against, not only do the logical circuits of the brain shut down, but there is an emotional high from rationalizing their current position. Not only will your best argument fail to influence, you will lose ground.

A study published in the *Proceedings of the National Academy of Sciences of the United States of America* in 2018 asked Republicans and Democrats to follow bots on social media with beliefs that contradicted their own, and after a month, they found the participants more entrenched in their views than before. Exposing them to other ideas did not open them up; it closed them down and pushed people further into their own preexisting beliefs. Simply trying harder or making a stronger argument not only doesn't work, it'll make things worse.

As you can see from Figure 1, as information and isolation have increased, receptivity continues to decline. And the experts respond, developing new and better selling strategies to convert the ever-shrinking percentage of customers who are willing to listen. As if to say, since there is less fertile ground, you need to get better at working with what you have. I think it's time for a new approach.

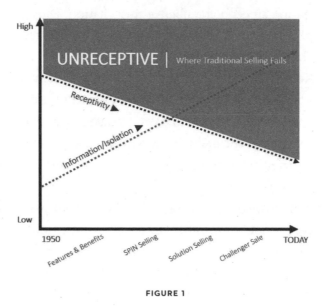

FIGURE 1

RECEPTIVITY > THE MESSAGE

Trying to persuade someone who is unwilling to talk will almost always backfire. Emotions, not truth, prevail, no matter how determined, smart, talented, or skillful you are. How, then, do we do the difficult work of prevailing upon a person whose ideas or opinions are wrong or different from our own? How do we achieve the very practical goal of hitting our quota? How do we get the prospect to say yes to a meeting?

As salespeople, we can easily ignore another person's receptivity to our message, putting all our energy and attention on the message. This often makes sales a one-dimensional form of communication. Since we are compensated for how well we convince another person, we often focus on just the message, but influence has two dimensions: the other person's receptivity (the soil) and the effectiveness of our message (the seed). When someone is not open to what we have to say, we need to stop selling entirely and focus on receptivity.

Maybe you already understood this, so you just intuitively backed off because you knew selling was a flawed strategy. Focusing on receptivity allows you to continue the dialogue and "plant" when the time is right.

There is more to this strategy than it'll-work-for-you-because-it-works-for-me. Everything in this book is backed by neuroscience, behavioral psychology, over twenty-five years of my own research and field testing, and the positive outcomes of the hundred thousand people my company has trained directly. There are deep, fundamental reasons why focusing on receptivity changes the climate of both the listener and the speaker and ultimately the outcome of their exchange.

For years, the traditional approach to selling worked. As long as you kept activity high, the failure rate was predictable, and the few wins were acceptable. Just keep making calls and delivering your pitch, and your quota was attainable. For most of us, though, those days are over and have been for quite some time. The customer and climate have forever changed, and today, receptivity is the key to building your pipeline, growing accounts, and closing deals. Not only will you hit your number, but selling will be easy and enjoyable.

Ultimately, this book is about achieving the highest level of influence and changing a person's beliefs. Of course, it will increase your sales, allowing you to be more successful and make more money. But it's about more than that. This book, if you let it, will help you persuade your friends, give feedback to coworkers, help your children see a better way, and advise loved ones who are struggling. You can use this power for good in all kinds of situations.

Receptivity is not about manipulating others so you can win the deal. It's about convincing them there is a better way to solve their problem. In the pages that follow, we will explore what few are able to achieve: becoming a trusted partner in the lives of others, influencing those who aren't open, changing the minds of those who think they have what they need, and ultimately earning a permanent seat at the decision-making table.

Most importantly, you will learn how to strengthen the one thing we all care about the most, which is our relationships. Yes, this is a book about sales, but if you embrace the insights and skills to come, and embrace the power of receptivity, you will improve how you relate to everyone in your life. Communication is the oil in the engine of all relationships, but most of what we've learned about it ignores the source of its breakdowns—another person's willingness to receive what we have to offer. In my life, after many failed attempts to change the people around me, I decided to consider others' openness before attempting to influence them in any way, and this choice changed every relationship in my life. What follows is an invitation for you to do the same.

HOW THIS BOOK WORKS

Although I hope you read the chapters in order, I understand as a seller the immediacy of needing to find the advice you want today. This book allows you to read each chapter as a stand-alone lesson for a particular situation. Whether you're aiming to effectively approach a new lead, trying to better engage an existing one, or hoping to make a new offer to a longtime customer, you can easily find the tools you need to succeed. There are five parts of the book, each addressing a unique barrier to persuasion: changing their perception of you, opening a closed door and getting a meeting, discovering the unfiltered truth, changing strongly held beliefs, and the willingness to take action.

In part I, we explore your mindset and why sales always starts with you. Without the right mindset, it is impossible to convert the Unreceptive. As you will see, the decisions you make before the meeting will determine what happens in the meeting. Once we've answered these questions, then, we have set the stage for escalating a prospect's receptivity and can move on. The rest of the book addresses the most important objectives in the persuasion process that determine how open or closed someone is to what we have to say.

In part II, we learn how to engage a prospect, what it takes to get their attention, and what to say when you do—in other words, how to get a meeting.

In part III, we learn to let go of our point of view, see things from another perspective, and uncover the unfiltered truth.

In part IV, we learn the most effective way to deliver our recommendation, address the customer's fears and concerns, and change strongly held beliefs.

And in part V, we address the barrier that ultimately determines if all your hard work has paid off: taking action. Here we explore how to ensure receptivity and help our prospects take the next best step.

This book is about the daily battles we all face in the epic war of opinions and emotions that pervade our lives. How do we change the mind of another person, someone we deeply care about and whose life we want to see improved? How do we help others see there is a better way? As with most things, it starts with us.

PART I

When we attempt to persuade, the first thing the customer "buys" is you. How you think about your role and your approach to selling will determine whether the customer buys you before they buy your recommendation. Therefore, receptivity starts with developing the right mindset.

If the number one barrier is customers' perception of you, the solution starts with us. Who we are communicates far more eloquently than what we say, so let's begin with developing the right mindset around the two fundamental drivers of receptivity: pressure and priority. To address the first barrier to converting an unreceptive audience, everything hinges on two questions asked consciously or subconsciously by every customer: "Are you going to pressure me?" and "Am I the priority?"

Your ability to move prospects from emotionally "closed" to "open" hinges on how you answer these two questions. It drives how you write an email, introduce yourself, learn what their needs are, deliver a recommendation, and advance the opportunity, whether that's getting another meeting, closing the sale, or helping them come to some other decision. In other words, the answer to these two questions determines everything.

So we start with developing a mindset that will almost instantly eliminate pressure and convince customers they are the hero of the story.

TWO

Drop the Rope

*In sales, there is always tension. And where tension exists, people
focus on the relief and not the truth. To end the tug-of-war, recognize
control is just an illusion and drop the rope.*

A vaccine representative for a major pharmaceutical company enters a meeting with a team of executives at the Mayo Clinic. The Mayo folks know the senior account executive's agenda—to convince them to prescribe more of the big pharmaceutical company's vaccines—and they're ready for it. The team is motionless. No questions, no emotion. The rep initiates a smattering of small talk, but his inquiries are met with brief answers. Impatience and obligation take up the oxygen in the room. Some of the rep's vaccines are needed by the Mayo Clinic, but their resistance is sky high. They expect an upsell. The conference table is more like a chess game with competitors staring across the table at one another as they strategize their next move. Mayo's unspoken message is clear: "Just tell us what we need to know about your vaccines and leave." What's the right move? Bear down and sell hard, or break the ice? Passionately deliver the prepared deck, or pivot into something more informal?

What would be *your* strategy?

YOU CAN'T MAKE ME

Because we are rewarded for what we sell, there will always be tension. You want them to buy, and they want to consider their options. When tension exists, people tend to focus on avoiding it. This was best illustrated in a five-second exchange in the classic TV show *M*A*S*H**. In just five words, the protagonist shows what happens when we look for results without first establishing receptivity. The scene involves Hawkeye Pierce, the chief surgeon, ignoring an order from his always inebriated boss, Henry Blake. Blake calls Pierce into his office and proceeds to yell at him, "Sit down, Hawkeye!" To which Hawkeye fires back, "You're forcing me to stand!" When we are told to do one thing, we almost instinctively want to do the opposite.

The moment makes an important point about human nature: we will do just about anything to resist being controlled by another person, the process starting for most of us when we are toddlers challenging our parents' authority. The need for control and choice is hardwired into our brains. In fact, research has found that people seek power not because they want to control others' actions but because they want to ensure their own autonomy. It's a survival mechanism.

Psychologists call this phenomenon "reactance." I call it the "Tug-of-War Principle." Whatever the name, it's an unpleasant arousal that emerges when someone experiences a threat to their free behavior. When a person tries to get us to do something, we feel as if they're "tugging" at us and instinctively "dig our feet" into the ground. We pull back. That's why, early in our marriage, when my wife used to tell me to put on my seat belt, I childishly refused, thinking to myself, "I would rather go through the windshield." This kind of resistance doesn't apply only to demands; it applies also to pressure, whether spoken or unspoken. When someone tries to get us to do something, even if it's in our best interest, we often naturally resist. To maintain a sense of urgency, we humans need to know we have choices and that we have a sense of ownership over those choices. The more others pressure us, the more it feels like they're trying to take away our choice.

People resist any outside pressure to think or act differently if they feel their choices are being limited. One study observed what happened when mock jurors were instructed to disregard certain evidence that reflected poorly on the defendant. If the judge gave a speech about why they must disregard the evidence, they were more likely to convict. As Ryan Smerek, organizational behavior expert at Northwestern University, put it, the "mock jurors reacted to being told what to think—to the degree that they decided to use the inadmissible evidence just to spite the judge for being spoken to authoritatively!" What should we do in situations like this when we are the perceived authority threatening to take away our audience's free will? We need to "drop the rope," relieving the tension so the others can see all their options, including but not limited to the solution we are offering.

Now let's get back to our pharmaceutical rep in the Mayo Clinic meeting room. What was his strategy? He dropped the rope, saying: "My goal today isn't to get you to sell more of our vaccines but to work together to solve a problem we both have: How do we get more patients to embrace the need for vaccines? Whether you buy more vaccines from us or the competition, my goal today is just to learn how we can work together to improve health outcomes. If we've burned too many bridges in the past, I understand. But my hope is that we can begin working together to solve a problem we both face. How does that sound?"

He addressed the tension in the room and communicated that he wasn't trying to pull them to his agenda. Instead, he was focused on their agenda, which was improving vaccines and health outcomes. He sent the message that it was their choice by asking permission and using words like *whether* and *if*. The tone of the meeting instantly changed, and for the first time in years, they met as partners instead of as combatants.

NOTHING TO RESIST

The Woodstock music festival was primed to be particularly violent in the summer of 1969. There were site issues, limited construction time, too many attendees, traffic delays, bad weather, a scarcity of food and medical supplies, and a sanitation crisis. The cultural movements at the time also increased conflict between hippies and law enforcement. Earlier that year, other big festivals in Miami, Denver, and Los Angeles had devolved into chaos because of similar issues. With all the tension in the air, Woodstock was likely to follow suit.

Security and law enforcement were worried, as they knew they needed order but also feared the kind of backlash such strict rules might cause in a crowd of rebels. They decided to do something different. Instead of bringing down the hammer even harder, they hired one of the crowd's own—entertainer-activist Wavy Gravy along with members of his Hog Farm commune—to handle the larger crowds. Wavy and his team created something dubbed the "Please Force," which took a very different approach. Instead of shouting orders like "Do this!" and "Don't do that!" they asked crowd members, "Would you please do this?" They didn't order them around; they asked. The volunteer security detail even set up "freak-out tents" where attendees who were experiencing bad psychedelic trips could ride it out.

People hate being controlled and told what to do, especially drugged-out hippies, but when you don't give them something to fight back against, it neutralizes the conflict. By not giving them anything to resist, Wavy Gravy's "Please Force" peacefully managed more than four hundred thousand people in one of the largest music festivals of all time. There were no laws but complete order, nonetheless. That's the power of dropping the rope.

"THANKS, I'M JUST LOOKING . . ."

Customers apply this concept of reactance even when a salesperson does nothing wrong. I've done it myself. Once, when needing a new television, I walked into Best Buy and was instantly overwhelmed with options. They all looked the same. Surrounded by giant screens with HD imagery and blaring sounds, I realized I hadn't done my homework and had no clue what I wanted. I was also in a hurry and had no time to figure it out. I needed help. An associate came up to me and offered, "Is there anything I can help you with?"

What did I say? "No thanks, I'm fine, just looking . . ." as if I preferred spending an hour reading little placards and comparing specs I didn't understand to talking to someone with the necessary expertise to help me get what I wanted in fifteen minutes. Why did I do this? The salesperson said nothing confrontational, but I rejected him nonetheless. I felt tense at his offer to help, an instant rigidity, because I assumed along with it came pressure. Many of us, without even realizing it, sense an affront to our independence is about to follow, so we reject any offer of "help" from someone who wants to sell us something. But at that Best Buy, on that day, what the salesperson did next changed everything.

"I don't get commission," he told me. "I'm just happy to help, so just let me know if you need anything." Then he started to walk away.

"Oh!" I replied, feeling a little desperate now. "Yes, please, I could use your help."

This savvy salesperson dropped the rope. Through his words and body language, he demonstrated that there would be no tug-of-war. We were not enemies; he was here to help and on my side. When he dropped the rope, all tension immediately lifted and I shifted from "closed" to "open." I became receptive. And I walked out that store a few minutes later with a brand-new TV.

Even though the Best Buy rep wasn't on a commission, the interaction demonstrates the power and ability to eliminate the preconceived tension that initially exists in every seller-buyer relationship.

TRADE THE ILLUSION OF CONTROL FOR INFLUENCE

Dropping the rope can feel impossible to salespeople because it means doing something we humans never want to do: relinquish control. But control is just an illusion. Influence starts by communicating the obvious—the customer has all the control. And by doing so, we trade the control we never had for the opportunity to influence.

When my business partner and I started our company in 1996, we knew we needed to join forces with another team that had expertise in the areas we lacked. We formed a partnership with a training and consulting firm run by two men, Ken and James, who had PhDs in behavioral psychology and had won awards for their innovative training simulations. After about six months, I became disenchanted with the relationship as we'd offered a sizable percentage of our intellectual property in return for sweat equity, and in my opinion, we weren't getting a lot of sweat. I reached out to schedule a meeting to talk through my concerns.

The meeting did not go well. We were working exclusively with Ken, but both he and James attended the meeting. As I communicated my concern, Ken got just a *tad* upset. They had years of experience running a successful firm, and we were just learning the industry. Their offices were on the top floor of a new high-rise, whereas we'd set up shop in my partner's basement. They were working with Fortune 500 companies. We had one contract with a local firm of about twenty-five employees. They had PhDs after their names, and we were, well, fun at parties. You get the picture.

Ken's frustration was reasonable. If the relationship was going to work, however, I needed to communicate my concerns, and it was clear my message wasn't being received. So I tried a different tactic. To substantiate their percentage ownership in the program, I slid our training book across the table and asked him to validate his contributions. He didn't exactly appreciate that move and left the room. Now, it was just the three of us. James wisely suggested we allow everyone to cool down and regroup in a week. We agreed and nailed down a time, and I spent the next seven days coming up with every conceivable reason to get out of the contract. I was not receptive to continuing our relationship with their firm, and in several imaginary conversations, I justified why we needed to end the relationship and that they should forfeit their ownership percentage. In the car, shower, and over dinner, I replayed the situation over and over in my mind.

The meeting date finally arrived. Due to scheduling conflicts, it was just James and me. I walked in with my speech all prepared, ready for battle, and James asked me to sit down on the couch. "It's some psychology trick," I thought, "and I'm not falling for it. I've brought my A-game today."

"Listen, Tom," James began, "obviously we can see you are uncomfortable with our partnership. The last thing we want to do is force you to continue in a relationship that's not best for you. So before we discuss your concerns, I want you to know that you have no obligation to work with us in the future. If you want out, that's totally fine with us."

After strategizing for a week about how I could shred the contract and pay them nothing, here's what came out of my mouth: "No, James, we don't want to do that. I'm sure we can figure out how we can continue to work together. We just need to get on the same page." Why the 180? When I no longer felt the pressure but instead the freedom to choose, I was able to reconsider what I wanted, which wasn't to end the relationship. My partner and I needed the expertise from this other team, and if I could trust them with determining an equitable relationship, the partnership was what I wanted. Dropping the rope is potent.

RELEASE THE PRESSURE

Teenagers are especially averse to even the slightest questioning of their choices, and there are scientific reasons why. "The rational part of a teen's brain isn't fully developed and won't be until age twenty-five or so," the University of Rochester Medical Center explains. Still, adults can be plenty irrational as well. We often remain unlikely to listen to concerns that fly in the face of how we feel about something, especially when those concerns involve the people we love. It's how we're wired.

At seventeen, my daughter had her first serious crush with some-one I had concerns about. What was I to do? Say nothing? As a father, I didn't see this as an option. But even if I told her, she'd most likely get furious at me, shut down the conversation, and potentially close the door to future conversations. The boyfriend—let's call him Stephen—met all the main criteria for the "popular crowd." He was a charming football player with Hollywood-good looks. But I wasn't sold. My son, her loving and protective older brother, played football with the boy and didn't approve either. I knew I needed to have a conversation with her. We went out for coffee, and after chatting for a bit, I brought up the subject: "Hey, tell me about Stephen."

"What do you want to know?" she said.

"How's your relationship? Why do you like him?" I asked in a calm, fatherly voice.

"We're good. He's good. Why are you asking?" She wasn't budging. The subject was closed.

"Great question," I said. "I would probably be a little suspect if my dad was asking me about my dating life. But here's what I want you to know: you can date whoever you want. My goal is not to keep you from dating Stephen. I just want you to be happy and especially don't want you to get hurt. So, if you want to date Stephen, date Stephen. As long as you abide by the rules of the house, it's your call."

Remember, at this stage, when those we desire to influence are emotionally closed, the goal is not to change their mind. The only goal is to move them to become receptive to discussing their options. By not challenging my daughter's freedom to choose, I gave her nothing to resist or defend. She didn't have to build a case to support her position because she didn't have to take a position. This allowed her to talk more freely, and she shared some of what she was thinking and feeling. I learned a lot too. She liked how being with this guy made her feel but had certain insecurities. She felt she couldn't measure up to her brothers: one was a music star and the other the quarterback of the football team. She wanted acceptance and felt this was how she'd get it.

Once her guard was down, I lovingly and without pressure shared what I had heard. After our conversation, she dated him a little while longer and eventually ended up breaking it off. A few years later, she told me how our conversation helped steer her in a better direction. This experience had long-term, positive consequences for the both of us, as it brought us closer together and improved all our communication. I traded my false sense of control for the opportunity to influence, and she slowly, over time, began to listen.

When we no longer demand someone to embrace our recommendation, they are more likely to agree with us. It's ironic, but it works. Dropping the rope allows you to shift the conversation from "I'm trying to sell you" to "It's your decision." By letting the person decide without pressuring them toward what we prefer, we are actually acknowledging reality: that, at any given moment, people are free to make whatever choices they'd like. But when you spell it out for them, it gives you both a framework for discovering the truth. When you let go of the tension and explore the options, you can see what's best. And if you're right that your solution really is the best one, the other person will likely discover it. Your goal is to offer an idea to be considered, not a path that must be chosen.

"You're seventeen. If you want to date Stephen, that's your call . . ."

"If you're not comfortable with the partnership, there's no obligation to continue . . ."

"I would love to talk with you about working with our firm, but I completely understand that it may make more sense to stick with _____."

When you use phrases like these, the pressure is released. Does this guarantee success? Absolutely not. What it does guarantee is a higher level of receptivity and the best chance to ensure the seed of your idea falls on fertile ground. Dropping the rope is counterintuitive; but once you get it, you'll find yourself using it everywhere. If you want your kids to heed your advice, make it optional. If you want customers to buy your solution, tell them the positive things about the competition. If you want to overcome an objection, agree with the customer's perspective.

This does not mean walking away from a conversation, losing your passion for what you're selling, or trying to lessen the impact of your recommendation. You can and should defend and promote the value of your solution, but don't tell customers what they should do or believe.

There's an art to maintaining this balance, one you'll develop through practices that we'll explore as we get into this book. Your job is to stay present in the conversation, committed to your beliefs, and confident in your recommended path without applying any force. Stay where you are and invite them to join if they wish. There's no coercion necessary.

IT STARTS WITH MINDSET

The simplest way to grasp the concept of dropping the rope is to list all the possible options the person you are attempting to influence has. For example, I was working with a team of software sellers whose sole responsibility was to upgrade their customers to the latest version. The goal was simple: persuade customers who were happy with the old version to spend more money on the new. One goal, one option. I asked them, "Other than upgrading to the latest version, how many options does the customer have?"

They looked as if I'd asked how they planned to jump off the Empire State Building. They couldn't answer, because the idea wasn't plausible. In their minds, there was only one choice: upgrade. As I began to push them a bit, they finally confessed the customer actually had four choices:

1. Upgrade to their more robust software application now.
2. Upgrade later. The upgrade may be needed, but due to other, more important priorities, now may not be the time to discuss or consider any changes to the current system.
3. Do nothing, as the current version meets the customer's needs.
4. Chuck the current software and buy a competitive program.

Guess which is the only acceptable option considered by the reps? Which option is promoted, measured, and rewarded by the sales leaders? There's only one acceptable outcome, so they make the call, and the tug-of-war begins. But people are smart; they naturally know there is more than one option even if the other option is simply to refuse whatever the salesperson is trying to sell them. The tension created by the rep is not intentional but naturally ensues when the customer is left with limited choices—in this case, only one. It's like a flight attendant saying to you on a long flight: "We have a wide variety of meal options for you: Would you like chicken or . . . chicken?" Dropping the rope boils down to allowing customers to freely explore all their options without limiting their choices to the few that benefit the rep.

"But what if my option is best for the customer?" the customer-focused rep may ask. "I just want what's best for my customers." Your motive may be pure, but when the customer's receptivity is low and you're only promoting option one, their preference for options two through four increases. As soon as you are the only solution, no one believes you. For the tension to release, dropping the rope can't be a manipulation tactic. Your motive must be to genuinely explore and consider all options.

HOW TO DROP THE ROPE

There are only two tensions that need to be resolved in the customer's mind:

First, "Am I free to talk later versus now?"

Second, "Is it okay if we explore alternatives outside the ones that benefit you?"

That's it. If you answer yes to those two questions, the rope is dropped, the tension is removed, and your chances of changing the customer's mind is higher. A simple way to ensure you successfully drop the rope is to follow a three-step process before every meeting.

Step One: Identify every path customers can take.

Not just your preferred path, but all the potential choices they have. All options fall within four categories:

1. Buy from you. Some form of your solution is exactly what they need.
2. Delay. The timing isn't right to consider your solution. Right now, there are other pressing priorities that need to be addressed.
3. Decide it's not a good fit. For the foreseeable future, your solution isn't relevant to their needs. They are selling their business or maybe just invested in a solution, and you are too late.
4. Buy from a competitor. They need a solution you offer but may decide a competitive offer is a better fit. You sell Audis, but they may believe a used Honda will work just as well.

Whether you like it or not, these are the four potential scenarios when pursuing a new or existing customer.

Step Two: Develop a plausible reason as to why all paths could be in the customer's best interest.

This is the step that will ultimately determine your ability to drop the rope. Recognizing that option one may not be in the customer's best interest ensures you are in the right frame of mind to drop the rope. When you consider how the customer may actually need a Honda, you will come across as genuine, because you *are* genuine. Another way to say it is if you are only interested in exploring option one, it is impossible to drop the rope. By the way, that's what customers already believe and why they typically avoid sellers. If you are always the only option, you can't be trusted. There just isn't only one car for everyone.

Step Three: Confidently communicate that all options are acceptable.

Early in the relationship, when little is known, you acknowledge that your solution may not be a fit. Even though you are stating the obvious, you are demonstrating that you are not a typical seller and this is a "no-pressure zone." If at some point in your meeting with the customer you become confident that the Audi is the perfect fit, you reinforce your willingness to talk about Hondas. Use language like *may, if, could be,* and *consider.* Avoid "allergic words" like *must, have to, can't,* and *should.* If you go through this process, you will be in the right frame of mind to drop the rope. Later, we will explore more specifically how to do this at every stage of selling so that you know practically what to do to become a trusted person of influence.

THE COMMON MYTHS

When first learning to apply this principle, I had major concerns about the negative outcome of letting the customer "off the hook." That's because I believed certain sales myths that needed to be addressed before I could take such a bold approach. There are four myths I grappled with that I still see sellers struggling to overcome.

Myth: My role is to sell my solution, and my solution only.

Truth: Yes, you are being paid to represent your company and sell your solution, but the truth about sellers in the top 1 percent is that they focus on helping the customer solve their problems and not just selling their solution. They place a higher priority on discovering the truth than on achieving a short-term win. This may include their solution, or it may not. But by being the customer's advocate, they sell more, and by recognizing that they can't effectively help the customer get what they want, they save countless hours pursuing unqualified opportunities.

To be clear, I'm not recommending you sell the competitive solution. What I am saying is by helping the customer explore the competitive solution, you are more likely to win. And if you recognize the competitive solution is what the customer really needs—a used Honda, for example—then you are free to serve someone else.

Myth: If I recognize all the customer's options, I'm sending the message that I endorse the wrong decision or the competitor's solution.

Truth: If you don't drop the rope, you are actually increasing the odds that they will make a bad decision. Dropping the rope is not about agreeing with their decision; it's about communicating that you believe the decision is theirs. Which is, of course, already true whether you say it or not. When you demonstrate a willingness to walk with them and explore all the options (consider a cheaper solution, delay the process, and so on), this changes the nature of the relationship. It is now safe for them to invite you into the decision-making part of the process and explore all the options with them, creating the opportunity for the highest level of influence. Dropping the rope earns you a seat at the table where you are invited into the decision making process, creating the opportunity for the highest level of influence.

Myth: Dropping the rope means not challenging the customer.

Truth: This is a common misconception. Dropping the rope doesn't mean you abandon your attempt to help the customer see the flaw in their strategy or change their beliefs. It's just about your approach. When you drop the rope, your objective is to help the customer make the best decision. As with doctors unwilling to challenge their patients' unhealthy decisions, passively watching them make a bad decision is malpractice.

Myth: If I play my cards right, I can control the customer's behavior and get the result I want.

Truth: You have no control in the situation. Even if you're absolutely certain your recommendation is best, the customer's decision is out of your hands.

Can you really stop your teenager from dating the wrong person?

Can you really force a customer to buy a product?

Can you really make your spouse stay on budget or convince someone in your family that what they're doing is unhealthy or get your team member to act differently?

No, of course not. Trying to control robs us of the very thing we desire most—to change someone's life for the better. Don't let the illusion of control rob you of the opportunity to influence. Later in this book, we will explore how to drop the rope when facing the barriers you encounter in each stage of the sales process.

THREE

Reset Your Compass

*The decision you make before the meeting ultimately determines
what happens in the meeting. Therefore, resist the gravitational pull
to self and reset your compass.*

In selling, there is always a strong gravitational current that, when left unchecked, will sabotage your ability to create receptivity. To avoid this instinct, you must make an important decision before you attempt to influence. Think about how you prepare for an important meeting. Maybe the outcome will result in a huge commission or determine whether you keep your job. Maybe it's meeting someone you love, and the outcome is critical to their well-being. Maybe you're a leader and need to talk with someone on your team about their performance. How do you prepare? What are the most critical questions you need to answer?

Why should they pay more for our solution?

Why is my firm the best company to solve their problem?

How do I prove my recommendation is in their best interest?

These are important questions that need answers, but they are secondary to the most important one, which is: Who is first? Obviously, you can't serve everyone. If you try to serve the wrong people, you will go out of business. But if it's worth the investment of time, there's one decision you need to make. Will you reset your compass and focus on who really matters?

SELLING IS SERVING

Early in 2020 as I was beginning to feel the financial pressures of the COVID-19 pandemic, I had a meeting with a Fortune 500 company that was interested in training a large, international sales force. The outcome could determine the financial well-being of our company. Would we have to lay off employees? Would I need to liquidate savings to support my family? Could something else go wrong that I hadn't foreseen? At the time, our current clients had put a hold on all scheduled work, and the marketing "faucet" had shut off on all incoming leads. We needed this sale.

We had gotten through the initial screening process, and now it was time to meet with the decision-making team. Since this was a global project, I set a meeting with the European partner and our senior consultant responsible for the relationship. We studied and debated our strategy. We discussed the competition and hidden decision drivers. We determined what responses should have the most weight and how to choreograph the meeting. What we didn't discuss was our intent. Was our goal to win or to serve?

Because the formal process was designed by the client and controlled by an outside consultant, we had very little information about the company. In retrospect, we were fuzzy about what they really needed and therefore unsure how or if we could help them reach their objectives. Most of the decisions we made about positioning our solution were based on guesses. But with pressure mounting, I threw all my energy and resources into figuring out how we could deliver a compelling argument for choosing our company.

Worried about delivering the perfect response, I was a little too rigid, missing some important clues about what was important to the customer. Most importantly, I didn't drop the rope. It was subtle but undeniable—even after studying this stuff for thirty years, every now and then I make the same fundamental mistake when the pressure is high. They decided to delay the project.

My underlying motive to win the deal drove the meeting and my response. When asked direct questions about why they should partner with us, I focused on our competitive advantage. I passionately communicated our experience and why I believe we offer the best training solution. In reality, I didn't know enough to answer the question: *Should they partner with us?* In retrospect, what I should have said was, "I don't know. I know very little about your company, what you need, and the resources you have in place. All I can tell you at this stage is why companies have hired us in the past, the solutions we offer, what we've learned over twenty-five years helping companies transform their sales organization, and the results we've produced for similar companies. For me to determine if we offer the best solution, our process is . . ."

I'm not saying I shouldn't have been passionate about the solution or about winning. I should be. You should be too. But those objectives must be secondary to our first priority, which is to serve. Not to sell, but to serve: because you are most successful when your focus is to help the customer solve their problem.

My assessment was confirmed by our internal team: "Tom, we offer a program called Other-Centered Selling, but you weren't other centered," they told me. *Ouch.* It stung, because it was true. It hadn't happened in years, but I allowed the pandemic and pressure to blind me to the most important aspect of influence: without stopping to determine my motive, I will always default to self. This doesn't make me a bad person; it just makes me less effective. My motive, and your motive, will eventually be telegraphed to the customer. Five out of five dentists have concluded: it's the number one cause of commission breath. And when we aren't aware of this default, we'll always fail to convert the Unreceptive.

RESETTING YOUR COMPASS

Driving home from the office a few weeks ago, I was hungry for a little mindless distraction. So I pulled out the Pandora app to enjoy my favorite comedian and received this message: "Someone else is listening to your Pandora account. Only one person can listen at a time." My wife and I share an account, which meant I had a decision to make. On the lower part of the screen, in bold blue, Pandora forced me to choose: "Let Me Listen" or "Let Them Listen."

There was no getting around it. I had to decide who was the priority: me or her. There are always only two options: you or them. When seeking to influence or sell, either you are the priority or they are. There is only one hero of this story, and you have to decide who it will be. Either your focus is to help them get what they want, or they are playing the part of helping you get what you want. Unfortunately, nothing pops up on the screen before a big client meeting, but if you don't make a conscious decision to hit the Them button, you will always default to self, which is an instinct critical to survival but will kill your chances of influence.

A compass works by recognizing the strongest magnetic force on the planet—the North Pole. Regardless of where you are, it highlights the direction you face in relationship to that central point. Each of us operates in much the same way in that our inner compass defaults to the strongest magnetic field in each of us, which is ourselves. Our lives really do revolve around us. If you sail into a meeting on autopilot, regardless of your beliefs, *you* will be the priority—not them, you. That's just how it works. Everyone has an agenda. You want to sell your stuff, increase the size of the deal, meet your goals, advance your career, pay your bills, and so on. Customers also have an agenda: they want to determine the best way to solve their problems, get a promotion, reduce stress, and so on. The problem isn't having an agenda; it's which agenda takes the top spot. And without being intentional about who is the number one priority, your agenda will win.

This is not an indictment on your character or mine. I know you would never consciously decide to place the highest priority on your commission. But by not consciously making a decision about your role, you automatically default to a self-centered agenda. By not making a decision, you've effectively already made one.

Because of our strong human instinct to survive, we default to taking care of self. On average, when not engaged in solving a problem, we think about ourselves about 95 percent of the time, according to Dale Carnegie's *How to Win Friends and Influence People*. When was the last time you had a dream and you weren't in it? Now you see my point. The key to avoiding this natural tendency is to reset your compass before every meeting. To avoid the default to self, we have to intentionally stop and choose to become what we call in my company other centered—that is, making a decision to place the highest priority on meeting the needs of those we've chosen to serve.

Regardless of your sales approach, we all have a self that likes to run the show. Receptivity begins with important and honest decisions, not behavior modifications. Like a rudder that determines the direction of a ship, our ultimate intent drives our behavior. And just as all athletes have a pregame routine to get prepared to perform, sellers need to stop and ask, "Who's first?"

Recently, I drove to Raleigh from Atlanta to meet with a top performer who has been with us for more than ten years. Candidly, I was worried we were losing him and wanted to invest in the relationship. His willingness to disclose concerns and receptivity to what I have to say about ASLAN does not begin at dinner that night; it starts on the four-and-a-half-hour drive. Who was this trip about: me or John? He will know if I am genuinely for him or just trying to keep our best guy around. He will know if the trip is just a manipulation tactic or if I truly care about him. Receptivity starts in the car, with me; it starts in the coffee shop before the meeting, before you click the Zoom link. It starts with an intentional decision to reset our internal compass; because what you do before the meeting will ultimately determine what happens in the meeting.

Other-centered sellers decide to set aside their agenda and what makes them feel comfortable, along with their own desires and goals, so that they can focus on meeting both the needs that relate to the solution they offer and a deeper, more important need as well. But before we dive into the customer's level of needs, and there are a few, it is important to answer an important question that people often wonder: Can you just fake it?

MOTIVE IS TRANSPARENT

I was coaching a seller last year and noticed an odd look on his face. I knew this person well. He was successful and well trained, but something was up. I could see it in his face and hear it in his tone. After the meeting, he admitted that he had a strong, negative reaction to the VP of sales, his potential customer. In fact, the VP was arrogant and condescending. The sales rep didn't like her, and it showed. Because he was aware of the need to be other centered, he attempted to hide his emotions, control his tone, and maintain a pleasant look on his face. But even his awareness failed to mask his inner feelings. He made the mistake we all make at times: he focused on behavior without resetting his compass.

Author and journalist Daniel Goleman explains that "the emotional mind sacrifices accuracy for speed, relying on first impressions." In his book *Emotional Intelligence*, Goleman cites studies conducted by Paul Ekman, a professor emeritus in psychology at the University of California, San Francisco, who is best known for furthering our understanding of nonverbal behavior. Ekman demonstrated that our faces ultimately can't hide our true emotions. We send subtle clues revealed in nuances in our facial expression that betray the beliefs and motives we intend to suppress. In fact, we have forty-three muscles in our face that can betray how we really feel and what we really want. The tone of our voice can communicate twenty-four different emotions. The point is there are too many ways that our voice, words, and facial expressions can betray our true intent:

"I need this deal. I'm well below my number."

"I'm going to push this product because it pays a higher commission."

"This guy is driving me crazy. He's asking way too many questions."

"I know the customer is taking a few shortcuts and this may bite them in the end, but I want to be liked."

The customer knows. When I remind my wife to wear sunscreen or encourage her to eat healthy food, am I worried about her health? I promise you my wife knows. If you are secretly striving for validation in your presentation, I assure you: your audience can see it. Are you more concerned about your children's welfare or your reputation as a parent? Your children know. Are you providing feedback because you sincerely want to help or because you want to establish yourself as a more competent person? The listener knows.

THE OTHER-CENTERED SELLER

Joe Max Higgins was in charge of the economic development for Mississippi's Golden Triangle area, a region in the eastern part of the state formed by the cities of Columbus, Starkville, and West Point and their respective counties. Before hearing that Japanese manufacturer Yokohama was looking to relocate its tire plant, he'd seen great success bringing roughly six thousand jobs—including half the area's manufacturing jobs—to the Golden Triangle since 2003. When he heard Yokohama was conducting a nationwide search for the right spot for its plant, he went right to work. As it turned out, there were approximately 3,100 locations Yokohama was considering. That's some stiff competition.

What would your plan be to convince the Japanese businessmen to choose your tiny town in Mississippi over the other 3,099 options? Would you focus on why your area was unique? Would you center your strategy on the return on investment? Would you put together a compelling PowerPoint presentation on your experience in working with manufacturers and "the ten keys that make the Golden Triangle the right choice for Yokohama tires"? If you were other centered like

Joe, you would think like the customer. Here was Joe's plan as captured on *60 Minutes*:

- He had all his employees learn about Japanese culture, and he
  personally studied up on tire manufacturing, so he could speak
  to Yokohama workers about the process.
- He reviewed competing communities' planning and zoning
  minutes and evaluated what competitive incentives he could
  offer.
- He also tracked the tail numbers of the company's private
  airplanes, so he could determine which competitor cities they
  were visiting and how long they were staying (because he knew
  that if they stayed somewhere longer it likely meant there was
  something they liked about the spot).
- He installed water and sewer systems on the proposed site for
  the plant and secured $30 million from the state for a new access
  road so trucks could reach the factory.

On the day the Yokohama chairman came to visit the Golden Triangle's prospective site, torrential rains had recently fallen. The thick
mud prevented Higgins from landing his helicopter on-site, and the
only alternative, landing on the road, was impossible with the flanking
power lines. Undeterred, Higgins asked the electric company to pull
down the power lines and asked the sheriff's department to block off
the road. Knowing how important this deal was to their slice of the
country, both complied. There was still, however, the issue of walking
the prospective site. Higgins didn't want his guests to ruin their dress
shoes in the mud, so he researched the shoe sizes for each member of
the Yokohama team and had galoshes ready for them. That's not all
the team saw when they arrived, though. Higgins also outfitted each
of his employees' vehicles with Yokohama tires.

Yes, Joe Max Higgins demonstrated the tenacity that all great sales
professionals possess, but what ultimately separated his solution from

the competition was his decision to be other centered. And in case you're wondering, he won over Yokohama. The Japanese company chose Higgins's site to relocate their plant, and they're still doing business to this day.

Higgins made a decision. The sales opportunity wasn't about him; it was about Yokohama, which meant he had to know what was important to his potential customers. He wanted to think and feel like they thought and felt. He anticipated their needs, understanding a critical key to driving receptivity: someone in the sales conversation is first, and if it's not the customer, receptivity dies. Higgins's entire approach centered on understanding what was important to the customer—from the actual site itself to the customer's culture and the size of their rain boots. You just can't fake that.

TWO TYPES OF SELLERS

Over several decades of interviewing thousands of sellers, I've noticed they tend to default to one of two approaches: the rep or the manager.

The rep's goal is to represent their solution. They primarily view selling as a competition and compete against other sellers in the organization or industry. The commission check, as one rep told me, "is equal to applause." This is why losing cuts deeper than just the loss of commission—it's personal. It's also why they hate to lose. Whether the driving force is their own ego, sense of self-respect, or financial gain, they want to achieve. Their loyalty is to their solution. In most cases, the goal is not to manipulate the customer, but to make a compelling case for their solution. The jury (that is, the decision-making team) decides what is right for them. It's a fair process, and the one who sells the most wins. Reps embrace the idea of serving the customer and meeting their needs, but under stress, the instinct to win can easily drive the show.

Then there are those who bristle at the idea of competing, who never have commission breath. In fact, they will do everything in their power to avoid the appearance of selling anything. These are the managers, those who are most comfortable managing and cultivating relationships. They love to educate and serve. They are loyal and resist making recommendations for fear of being categorized as one of "those people." They default to letting the customer lead.

On the surface, this appears to be a very customer-centric approach: no pushing, no pressure, no manipulation. Everyone is happy, right? This is true if the customer knows all and/or has unlimited amounts of time. When, however, was the last time you met with customers who had a complete understanding of their problem, along with every aspect of the solutions offered? Even if they had the expertise, which is rare, they won't have the time to vet all the options. In reality, if you default to letting customers lead, they will get lost and likely make a poor decision.

While their behaviors look different, both the rep and the manager can easily default to self. One can appear pushy, manipulative, and myopic, whereas the other may avoid potentially uncomfortable conversations by simply refusing to go there. The manager reacts and places a higher priority on the relationship than challenging and leading the customer to the best solution, which is in its own way selfish. If you are an expert in your field and your job is to help people solve a specific problem, then you need to lead. If not, by default the customer bears the burden of figuring it all out.

The failure of the seller to own the problem, offer valuable expertise, and effectively lead the customer is a primary reason why a customer's desire to engage with sellers when evaluating a solution has dropped 120 percent from 2016 to 2019. In a study of customers buying business-to-business solutions in 2016 conducted by McKinsey & Company, 18 percent of customers preferred a self-service model when evaluating a solution. By 2019, that number had increased to 61 percent. The interaction with a seller is either too painful or just plain unhelpful. They would just rather figure it out for themselves. The problem is: they won't.

If you tend to think and operate like a manager, you may need to reset your compass by deciding not to sell but to proactively lead customers to the best solution to *their* problem. This will help you shed the negative associations with selling and elevate your role to serving at the highest level. If you, like me, have the DNA of a rep, consider reframing your win as getting the customer to see the truth. If you do and choose wisely, you will win far more deals by making the customer the hero of the story.

THREE LEVELS OF NEEDS

In sales, think of needs in terms of three levels, from least important to most important: stated solution needs, unstated solution needs, and emotional needs. Solution needs relate to the problem your product, service, or solution solves. The greater, deeper need is more emotional; it's what makes us all feel a deep sense of meaning, connectedness, and validation. Other-centered sellers focus on meeting all the customer's needs.

Solution Needs: Stated and Unstated

All customers you meet have stated and unstated needs related to the solution you offer. Stated needs are their perceived needs—what they think they need. Unstated needs are needs being overlooked by the inexperienced buyer. For example, maybe you sell insurance and a client wants to buy $500,000 worth, but based on what you know the client really wants, that amount would leave the person underinsured. Or maybe you sell real estate, and the buyer is in love with a house but unaware that the house is in a poor school district. Maybe you sell a solution like software, and the potential customer is focused on automating a key part of their business but has completely overlooked a critical part of solving their problem—employee adoption. These are all examples of stated and unstated solution needs. Other-centered sellers focus on meeting both, but they also understand and strive to meet an even greater need.

Emotional Needs

Emotional needs are drastically different from solution needs and never revealed; yet they drive almost everything we do and care about. Maslow was right: once our need to survive is met, our greatest need is emotional. And understanding this emotional need is the secret to understanding what makes every relationship work, why people are or are not drawn to you, and ultimately your ability to influence.

Pause and think about your most important relationship. Who is it with? The health of that relationship does not depend on how attractive or beautiful you are. It does not depend on the financial security you provide. It does not depend on how talented, funny, or intelligent you are. This relationship doesn't even depend on who you are but how well you meet that person's greatest need. There is a LAW that governs every relationship, and if you understand this, you will always be the most attractive person in the room; and your relationships will flourish.

Let's break down this acronym to explore what that looks like and how understanding each one drives your relationship and ultimately the person's receptivity.

[L]OVE = CHOSEN

The word *love* has multiple meanings, as in, "I love you, bro," or "You are the love of my life," or "I love that shirt." The best way to think about this word, then, in a way that applies to all relationships, is to define it as the need to be chosen. Whether being chosen by our parent or spouse as their number one priority, or being part of a select social group, we all want to be chosen. Which is to say we all want love.

(A)CCEPTED = LIKED

The comedian Kevin Hart captured this idea well when he said, "Acceptance is a drug as powerful as crack." We are all acceptance magnets. When you walk into a room, without your even thinking about it, your feet point you in the direction of the people who want to be around you. We are all drawn to people who like us and who are like us. These relationships aren't dependent on holding back and denying our authentic selves. They are why we seek out people with similar personalities and backgrounds and why, when meeting a stranger, we search for common ground, saying things like, "Where are you from?" "What do you do?" "Do you have kids?" We intuitively know that finding similarities is a connecting point.

This doesn't mean we are drawn only to people with the same personality. Differences can and should be seen as strengths. Regardless, what drives our desire to be with another person is acceptance. They smile when we walk into the room. They value and accept our unique qualities. And we like this. And when we get it, we want more of it.

(W)ORTH = VALUE

Lastly, we want to know that our unique talents, thoughts, and opinions are valued. We want to know we have something of value to offer. This is why I saw a mom in her late forties practicing tennis late at night one night—we all want to be good at something. This is why it cuts a little deep when someone we barely know snubs us or ignores our opinion. And it is why blowing a presentation stings more than the mere loss of a commission. It's also why even the most successful people in the world ask Oprah after appearing on her show, "How did I do?" We all want to matter.

Think about how children will literally scream for attention: "Watch this . . . Did you see that?" They want to be noticed, told they are okay. They unashamedly seek to know if they matter. When we get older, regardless of our cool exterior or how much we've accomplished, the need doesn't change. We know it's not acceptable to vocalize our need for love, acceptance, and worth, but it drives almost everything we do.

This explains why we all love puppies.

Influence Begins with How You Make Them Feel

Is it our role in sales to meet all these needs? Are you supposed to love your customers? Not in the romantic sense, of course. But what is important in sales is that people are drawn to you based on how good you make them feel. We let them know that we've chosen them by remembering what is important to them, how they like to communicate, or important personal information shared. We accept them by genuinely liking who they are, the qualities that are as unique to them as their fingerprint. We communicate their worth by valuing what they value and their contribution to every conversation.

Think of it this way: when people have the three emotions triggered, the dopamine centers of their brain light up. People get "high" when they are around those who love to be with them, listen to their stories, and heed their advice. Conversely, we go to great lengths to avoid others who demonstrate the opposite—those who are condescending, interrupt our stories, monopolize the conversation, and give us the "look" when we say or do something that doesn't meet their approval. Getting this need met produces the emotion that we all crave and want to feel. Think about how the Like button and being tagged in a photo has driven the explosion of social media. We instantly feel chosen, accepted, and valued when people follow us or like or compliment our post.

In the book *Compelling People*, authors John Neffinger and Matthew Kohut spent years researching what makes someone compelling. These are people we want to be with, people we listen to, people we follow. The authors simplified what makes someone compelling down to two primary traits: they are warm and strong. What makes someone warm? How well they meet other's emotional needs. In short, compelling people are other centered.

It doesn't matter if you're an introvert or extrovert. This isn't about your DNA or whether you are a people person. When you are around people, their brain either lights up with positive emotions or it doesn't. Other-centered people have this superpower. Because they understand it isn't about their needs but about the other person's, they understand the best way to get their needs met is by focusing on others. My goal in this section is to establish the right mindset. Before every meeting, other-centered people make a decision to set their agenda aside and reset their internal compass to focus on the customer's solution needs (stated and unstated) and their emotional needs.

A relationship is almost always a choice, whether that's a parent choosing a child, a romantic partner pursuing a marriage, or a seller choosing to pursue a customer. And most people cannot resist unconditional love and acceptance, those who value their contribution to the world. If you have the opportunity and focus on the laws that drive relationships, in time you will win over that person. It won't be a perfect relationship or even the exact relationship you want, but you will create a strong connection. And you will build a foundation to be heard.

Throughout the book, we will talk more specifically about how to meet the customer's needs and how to shed light on the truth that people buy you before they ever buy your recommendation. Here the focus is on the decision to put the customer's needs first—all three levels of needs. Receptivity starts in the heart. Without pausing to reset your compass, your filter will break down and your true motive will be revealed.

OTHER CENTERED IS NOT SELFLESS

I'm not asking you to remove your needs from the equation; I'm recommending you make them secondary to the customer's needs. Why? Because it's in your best interest to put others first. In short, you will sell more.

In my thirty years in sales, those who are other centered, and have a dedicated work ethic, will always beat a self-centered sales approach. Always. Are there self-centered reps who outsell other-centered reps? Absolutely. A proactive rep with a strong work ethic will always catch more fish than a talented, other-centered rep who rarely wets a line. But if two sales reps with the same drive and work ethic go head-to-head for the same opportunity, my money will always be on the other-centered rep.

You don't need to serve everyone. In fact, when you try to serve everyone, you will serve no one. We can't treat everyone equal—it's impossible. But if you choose wisely (more on this in chapter 15) and make a decision to be other centered, you will reach your highest potential.

DEVELOPING THE RIGHT MINDSET: ARE YOU OTHER CENTERED?

The sales professionals who are most successful at ensuring a high level of receptivity all share a common characteristic: other-centeredness. They value, live, and sell in a way that rebels against the self-centered norm. This shift in priority leads to a shift in behavior that elevates them well above the typical seller. But with such a strong magnetic pull to self, how will you know if you are genuinely other centered? Here's how:

- The desire to talk is replaced with the desire to hear.
- The desire to chase is replaced by the desire to help.
- The temptation to bend the truth is replaced by candor.
- The need to control is replaced with a need to communicate the freedom to choose.
- The need to win at all costs is replaced by a concern that the customer makes the best decision.
- The frustration of working with a difficult decision maker or dealing with people who are "in your way" is lessened, and empathy wells up as you attempt to understand their challenges.

- The fear of failure is superseded by the need to ensure the customer makes the best decision.

By answering these questions, you can determine if you have the right mind to engage the customer. Now, with the two fundamental drivers to receptivity—pressure and priority—addressed, it's time to shift gears and get practical. In the next part, we will look at how to engage the most unreceptive prospects, discover their needs, and build in value when the odds of winning are extremely low.

PART II

Now with the groundwork laid, being other centered and dropping the rope provide a foundation for how to navigate the barriers you will face at each stage of the sales process: engaging the decision maker, discovering needs, delivering your recommendation, and advancing the opportunity. In part II, we begin, for most, with the most difficult step: opening a closed door. Here, more than at any other stage, sellers need to deny their instincts, challenge conventional wisdom, and do what no other sales professionals are doing.

FOUR

The RAS and the Power of Your Position

Sellers fail to engage decision makers more than 98 percent of the time for one simple reason: they don't know how to position a meeting. Therefore, change your position and prospecting gets easy.

Influence begins with a commitment to meet. Changing beliefs does not happen in a hallway conversation, in an email, or a brief phone conversation. In sales, this is the greatest receptivity barrier. Whether trying to expand your reach in an existing account or trying to engage a cold prospect, this is often the toughest step. Where do you begin?

You're about to write an email, or maybe you're one of the remaining few who still uses phone calls for prospecting. Perhaps, if you are a little creative, you develop a video, maybe even send a LinkedIn message. You could even decide to go "old school" and send a package with a handwritten note. And when you reach yourself, what do you lead with:

- Your best product?
- Your most compelling benefit?
- A case study with some impressive ROI?
- The mysterious "you don't know why I'm reaching out, so you will have to respond to find out" strategy?
- A mutual interests approach?

No. Scratch all of those. Sellers fail to engage new decision makers more than 98 percent of the time for one simple reason: they don't know how to position the meeting. This is also why we hate prospecting. It's like a ninth-grade boy in high school trying to get a date—just a whole lot of rejection. At this stage, receptivity is low, and the rejection rate is high. Creating a relationship out of thin air in less than thirty seconds is not for the faint of heart. It not only requires mindless repetition but often a little groveling. Does it have to be this way? Not if you decide to set up the meeting differently, which starts with understanding a part of your brain called the reticular activating system (RAS).

My wife and I were visiting our daughter at college one weekend, and I had to finish a proposal that was due on Monday. Not wanting to lose a minute of quality time with my fam, I got up early Saturday morning and headed down to the hotel lobby, settling for an out-of-the-way corner and trying to ignore the TV on the other side of the room. For about an hour, I focused on work and was able to tune out the noise—until one commercial grabbed my attention.

"These tires are more durable than all others," the voice said. "It's impossible to get a flat tire." The man's words yanked me into a state of attention. How did that specific sentence from that particular ad break through my concentration? Why do we ignore 99.9 percent of the messages we encounter every day but notice one or two that break through the clutter? The answer lies in understanding how the RAS works. This is key to getting the attention of prospects and explains why the average response rate to introductory sales emails is less than 3 percent and appointments set through cold-calling efforts average less than half a percent.

THE RAS

Located at the base of your spinal cord is a complex collection of neurons that serve as a point of convergence for signals from the outside world. This is the RAS: an automatic mechanism that brings relevant information to your attention, acting as a filter between your conscious and subconscious mind, dampening down the effect of repeated stimuli such as loud noises, and preventing the senses from being overloaded.

Today, more than ever, our RAS is working overtime. Think of the amount of information coming at you on a daily basis—text messages, email, social media, internet, signs, and ads on every surface you see. As I mentioned in chapter 1, our brains are processing thousands of messages a day. Most go unnoticed by your conscious mind, but some make it through. Which messages get noticed and which information gets relegated to the junk folder?

That's the job of the RAS.

How does this triage occur? At any given moment, the RAS recognizes, stores, and catalogs all the information our brain is receiving. This allows you to go about your day until the RAS is triggered and signals, "Hey, you need to pay attention here." Even though I consciously tuned out the television, my RAS was monitoring the outside world. Like a friend who sees the car in your blind spot, it tapped me on the shoulder and said, "Hey, Tom, pay attention!" Why did my RAS care? Because I've had five flat tires in the last three years. That's right: *five*. Information on how to avoid more flat tires was clearly something my frontal cortex needed to know about.

Think about the last time you were in the market for a car. On the way to work, what did you notice? Probably every car that fit the type you were considering. You didn't have a pep talk with your brain one day and say, "Hey, listen, as we're driving to work, look for German SUVs. I know you normally zone out, but today, stay focused on German SUVs." No, you just hopped in your car, started driving, and your brain subconsciously went to work. Once you made the decision that you were in the market for a new car, every car that met your criteria caught your attention. The same holds true for emails, voice mails, or uninvited phone calls. If they aren't RAS-worthy, they will be ignored.

The RAS has two simple requirements: it is always looking for either a known problem or anything disruptive. Early on, the frontal cortex had a meeting with the RAS and gave it clear instructions. "Listen, it's getting pretty crowded up here and I need some help. There are only two things I want you to bring to my attention: (1) anything I need (avoid flat tires) or (2) anything I don't understand or is out of the ordinary. If you're not sure what it is, let me know and I'll check it out. After all, what we don't know could kill us." That may not be how they teach it at Harvard Medical School, but you get the idea. Understanding this reveals an important truth about prospecting: it's not about selling; it's about alignment. Your goal isn't to create a need or pitch your solution but to tap into a need that already exists. As David Ogilvy, founder of one of the most successful ad agencies in the world, said, "If you sell fire alarms, start with the fire."

The second filtering criteria is equally as important as the first. Think about the last time you flew. Did you pay attention to the scripted preflight announcement about seat belts and so on? For those of us that fly a lot, we tune it out because we've heard it before, subconsciously thinking, "Nothing new here." We go back to our email, texts, newspaper, or whatever is currently capturing our attention—unless there is a really creative flight attendant.

On a recent flight, I heard on the intercom: "Most people tune out during the safety bit. I don't want to be that guy, but I just hope you will be okay. That's all I am saying." Why did I suddenly tune into an announcement I had ignored for years? Because it was unexpected. This underscores the importance of the second filtering criteria. What's different gets noticed. Predictability determines impact. Everyone is sending emails about their stuff. Blah, blah, blah. To get noticed, you must break away from the norm. Think for a moment about what your prospects are expecting:

- They will receive a canned, generic message about your company and your solution.
- You don't know anything about them.
- You have no expertise to offer.
- You lack unexpected insight on how to address their unique problem or need.
- You will bend the truth to get a meeting.

You want to get noticed? You want to engage the more than 90 percent of people who aren't receptive to a sales call? Pay attention to the RAS. Understanding how this part of the brain functions sheds light on how to succeed at the first requirement of successful prospecting, which is developing your position.

Over the last decade, I've studied the most effective emails, cold introductions, ads, and billboards. Whether they're selling software, insurance, industrial tools, or plastic surgery, they all have something in common. There is a predictable formula all persuasive copy follows, which is good news because it means such success can be repeated.

Effective persuasion always starts with developing your position. Your position is the heart of your message. It distills the purpose of your call or email down to just a few sentences that answer the question "why meet?" Once the position is developed, you can deliver it in multiple mediums: live introductions, email, voice mail, LinkedIn, and so on. The first step to breaking through the noise, however, is to learn a framework to develop a RAS-worthy message. Before we look at a framework designed to help you develop your position, it's helpful to break down the steps to breaking through the noise and improving your response rates.

STEP ONE: GET THEIR ATTENTION BY FOCUSING ON THEIR POINT OF VIEW

In 1998, Monster.com was a fledgling startup with less than $50 million in revenue. They had a bold plan to replace the yellow pages and become the leading job site online. Much like Apple's launch of the personal computer, they chose the Super Bowl as their coming-out party. It worked. In thirty seconds, Monster.com was a known brand, going on to win *Time* magazine's ad of the year award. More importantly, their quarterly revenue doubled overnight, reaching almost a billion in annual revenue by 2012.

Why was the ad so successful? How would you have positioned their service? Easy to use, the most inexpensive or effective way to find talented people? Their central message had nothing to do with their service but everything to do with us. The ad featured kids sharing the antithesis of what we all aspire to do in our career: "I want to be a brown nose . . . I want to climb to middle management . . . I want to file all day . . . I want to be a yes-man, a yes-woman." In thirty seconds, they found a clever way to say what we all really want: to be who we dreamed we would be. And more importantly, they activated the RAS of their target audience by describing their problem, the need for a better job.

This is where we should begin when developing our position: resist the temptation to talk about yourself and instead make the prospect the hero of the story. Leading with your solution would just be white noise. Start with what's on their "whiteboard."

Here's what I mean by that: Picture the person you are about to engage. See them sitting at their desk or cubicle and imagine a whiteboard in their office. What's on it? If you want to get someone's attention, don't talk about you, your solution, or even attempt to invent a new creative approach. Just lead with what's on their whiteboard.

"Their whiteboard" is just a metaphor to describe the customer's point of view, a term we will explore throughout the remainder of the book. Point of view is simply defined by what the customer cares about most and includes three categories of information: (1) what *they* want (their desired destination), (2) *their* perspective on the best way to get what they want (their plan), and (3) challenges *they* face in implementing the plan (their problem). To effectively answer the question "why meet?" and get a response, you can focus on any one of the three. At times, it may be more effective to lead with what they want (for example, "Because your goal is to double the number of offices in California."). Or, because of what you sell, you should lead with their perspective. For example, if they believe your solution doesn't work, lead with that. But odds are, the most compelling is number three—a recognized problem, and the more specific you are, the better.

Regardless of what you choose, here's the truth: If I show you a picture of yourself, you will look at it every time. If I show you a picture of me, you will probably ignore it, especially if I'm a stranger. The other day, I got an email that began with the title of an article I wrote. The seller showed me my "picture," and I immediately looked at it. That's how the RAS works.

If you lead with anything related to a client's point of view, the RAS will spot it like a kid passing a candy aisle. For example, if you were sitting in my office during the writing of this book, you would see the outline of the entire book, chapter by chapter, on my whiteboard. This explains why I opened a recent email titled "Finishing a Book." Any message, in any form, that involved something on that board— publishing a book, writing a book, selling a book—would be irresistible.

The RAS is a tough filter. It takes instructions very literally. Like when interviewing for a job: you are unknown to the prospective employer, and the best way to get in the door is not to change the hiring criteria but to *be* the criteria. This holds true for prospecting as well: changing beliefs about what solution is needed happens once you are in the door; but until then, we need to align with a problem on their whiteboard. If you sell IT services and on the prospect's hypothetical whiteboard under action items it says, "reach out to IT services," it's easy. An email that says, "Hey, are you looking for IT services?" will get their attention. But for the other 98 percent who don't have that on their whiteboard, the email is unread and deleted. To convert the disinterested, you need to lead with a problem that requires IT services. The more specific the description, the higher the probability that your message will be noticed. For example, instead of saying, "Companies that are expanding often struggle with . . . ," say, "As you plan to open up seven new locations in the Midwest . . ." The second message can't be ignored. The RAS demands it.

An agent for Rick Warren, author of the number one *New York Times* bestselling book *The Purpose Driven Life*, wanted to meet with the president of NBC. Talk about a tough cold call. The objective was to create more awareness of the book by being featured on *Dateline NBC*. What would you lead with? Impress them with the number of books sold? It is one of the highest-selling books of all time. How about pitching the importance of everyone on the planet wanting to know why they are on a big rock floating in space? That's good programming. The rep didn't do any of that. He ignored what he thought would be compelling and shifted focus to what was on the president of NBC's whiteboard—how to stop the consistent loss of the conservative audience. His central position: if you want to attract the audience you are losing, book Rick Warren. Sold.

Does leading with the customer's point of view guarantee a response? No, we will discuss that in steps two and three. What I'm promising here is to get noticed. You may be thinking, "But what if you don't know what's on the prospect's whiteboard?" One option is to identify an insider, or you may think of it as a coach. An "insider" is someone who is not part of the decision-making process but understands and experiences the problem your solution addresses, and is therefore typically motivated to help. They are also close enough to the decision makers to provide information about their whiteboard. This is obviously the best source for information but requires a significant investment of time.

For less qualified opportunities, focus on what people in similar roles have on their whiteboards and make an educated guess. What are their top three challenges? What can you learn about the person, the role, or the company on the web?

If you know nothing about the person or the role you are attempting to reach, stop prospecting and go to school on the decision makers you serve. Sometimes you need to slow down to speed up. Or be prepared to live with a less than 2 percent success rate. Here are a few questions I've found helpful in gaining a deeper understanding of my customers' worlds:

- What are the top three challenges they face in their role and industry?
- How do they earn their bonus? How is success in their role defined?
- Who are the top two or three thought leaders they respect/listen to? Why?

- What trade shows do they attend? What industry publications do they read? It's helpful to grab a trade show program and read through the list of topics. This will tell you what's top of mind for attendees.
- What are the four or five things they must do well to be successful in their role?
- What are their top three to five initiatives for the upcoming year?
- If I sent them an email, what would get their attention?

If calling a current list of clients isn't an option, add a couple of questions to every meeting you have with decision makers. In a brief period, you won't have to wonder what's on their whiteboard. You will have the information you need to activate the RAS.

There's one more benefit of leading with a problem or need on decision makers' whiteboards. Not only does it grab their attention; it says something about you. This approach demonstrates you are the rare person, especially for a salesperson, who is more interested in others than themselves. These are the type of people that strangers will meet with and give away a precious hour of time. Once we identify the problem, the second step is to strengthen our message by communicating something the prospect doesn't know about solving that problem: a disruptive truth.

STEP TWO: BUILD CREDIBILITY BY SHARING A DISRUPTIVE TRUTH

Decision makers don't meet with sales reps. They delegate the tasks of sifting through vendors to someone else. So how do you tackle one of the most common obstacles to prospecting? Don't be the typical sales rep. Offer a disruptive truth about a better way to solve their problem or get what they want.

Think about it this way: If you were speaking at a conference to a room full of decision makers, what tidbit of wisdom, best practice, or principle could you share that would be so surprising and important that everyone would write it down? For that to happen, you'd need to avoid focusing on your solution but share unknown insights about the best way to solve their problem instead.

This pearl of wisdom is the most compelling information you can share in an email, introduction, LinkedIn message, voice mail, or from a conference stage. It elevates your value and moves you from a seller-of-stuff to someone who might be worth meeting.

The book *The Challenger Sale* studied the most successful sales professionals and discovered a common denominator: they win by sharing unknown insights, teaching customers a better way to solve their problem. Customers are looking to suppliers to challenge their thinking and enlighten them about the best way to solve their problems. The lack of this kind of feedback is why most decision makers don't meet with sales reps. Why would a decision maker who works a fifty- to sixty-hour-per-week job read something from a sales rep? For only one reason—you know something the person doesn't. If you do, the RAS pays attention. To get a meeting, you need to develop disruptive truths.

Disruptive messages attack conventional wisdom. If what was previously considered true is a lie, the RAS is activated. For example: "Lose weight by eating donuts." If a prospect wants donuts (donuts are definitely on their whiteboard), then this truth is very compelling. The brain needs to know why the world works differently than it previously believed. Here are a few disruptive truths that recently captured my attention and compelled me to lean in:

- If you want to save more money, increase your charitable contributions.
- The quality of your service or product doesn't determine customer loyalty.
- People don't read websites—they scan them.
- You are never happier than your relationships.
- Your passion is actually the source of your suffering.
- People who are attempting to motivate you to work an eighty-hour week aren't teaching you to become an entrepreneur. They are teaching you how to get a divorce.

These statements are either counter to conventional wisdom or offer a disruptive insight. And because the information was unexpected, they made it through the filter. As you think about constructing your disruptive truths, focus on communicating them as definitive facts, laws, or principles. Consider Simon Sinek's talk on "How Great Leaders Inspire Action," which was the basis for his bestselling book *Start with Why*. It has become one of the top TED Talks ever delivered and has been viewed more than fifty million times. He shared a disruptive truth on what really motivates people to buy a product or service. It's unconventional; it's not what people expected. "People don't buy what you do," he famously said. "They buy why you do it; and what you do simply proves what you believe."

The idea that your "why" drives more sales than what you offer is radical. "Find people who care about the why and not the what" was a disruptive truth, and it stuck. This is why Sinek has over two and a half million followers on LinkedIn and how he became a bestselling author and sought-after speaker. Also, notice how he delivered this idea: as a definitive fact and with complete certainty. Delivering a new truth not only grabs the listener's attention but instills confidence, inspires action, and sends a message to the decision maker that you are more than a sales rep—you are a resource. Your value goes up as do your engagement rates. Additionally, sharing a disruptive truth enhances receptivity. You are sharing unknown wisdom that helps your listeners solve their problem with no commitment on their part required.

Let's look at three examples from Braintree, a division of PayPal. Here's how they position their online payment solution to companies selling products over the web:

"For every second of delay at checkout, conversion drops 7 percent."

"Up to 68 percent of online carts are abandoned before checkout."

"Forty-two percent of millennials limit their own mobile transactions because of security concerns."

In one sentence they described customers' problem (losing shoppers at checkout; that is, low conversion rates) and shared a disruptive truth. Unlike Simon Sinek, they focus on statistics to tell the story instead of principles. Both strategies are effective. Again, the key is to state the truths as a fact, and the more counterintuitive the message, the more effective. Articulating a relevant problem and communicating a disruptive truth will get you noticed and establish credibility, but one more step is needed to get more meetings. To engage, we need to offer a unique solution to the problem.

STEP THREE: CREATE CONTRAST BY COMMUNICATING A PROPRIETARY BENEFIT

To move the prospect from clicking to responding, from listening to calling, you need to communicate a proprietary benefit. Related to the problems your solution was created to solve, what do you own? What can only you offer? Whether it's what you offer, your price point, or how you deliver your solution, what differentiates you from the competition or from internal solutions available to the prospect? Whether it's a what, a who, or a how, if you own it and they need it, you are making a compelling case to engage.

Let's make it more personal. Imagine you are being recruited for a sales role at a respected company. It's your dream job. They are the market leader and offer a killer comp plan. It's obviously competitive. Hundreds of candidates are applying for the job. So why should you get it? What differentiates you from all the other candidates? If you can't quickly articulate the answer, you won't get hired. The same holds true in prospecting.

Have you created a list of your proprietary solutions and the unique benefits they offer? Not a list of everything you offer but only the ones that can't be obtained anywhere else in the world by the customer or competitor? If not, develop a list of the proprietary solutions you offer and the benefits of those solutions. If the competition can tell the same story or it's very difficult to create contrast in the mind of the prospect, scratch it. What do you offer that differentiates you from the competition? Whether it's what you offer or how you deliver it, communicate that.

Think about how you would attempt to convince someone to try your favorite restaurant, hotel, or product. You can easily distinguish your chosen restaurant from all the others. You have chosen to represent this solution. Why? Identify that! It's the source of your passion and why people believe what you believe. I'm certainly not recommending the use of cheesy phrases like "best ever" but I am suggesting you identify and learn to articulate what differentiates you from the competition.

Remember to avoid the features and focus on the unique benefit you offer. The goal here is to create an interest in knowing more. Once you engage, you will have time to answer questions related to how the benefit is delivered. Your goal is to separate yourself from all the other sellers who are sending lengthy, boring emails filled with laundry lists of stuff that no one cares about, least of all the decision maker.

How many proprietary benefits should you communicate? If you offer your favorite five, you will lose the prospect. As James Carville, a hired political consultant, advised Bill Clinton when running for president, "If you say three things, you say nothing." To stand out, take a stand. A watered-down message has no impact. Choose only one. If after a few attempts you fail to get a response, you can switch it up.

OTHER-CENTERED POSITION FRAMEWORK

Now that we've unpacked the steps to effectively position a meeting, let's bring it all together in one framework: the Other-Centered® Position. You can see by looking at Figure 2 that if you follow this process, combining their point of view with a disruptive truth and adding your proprietary benefit, you create an impossible-to-ignore Other-Centered® Position (OCP). Here are a few examples to get you started on developing your OCPs. I'll start with a hypothetical example from a company I'm familiar with and is germane to your role as a seller—Salesloft, a provider of sales engagement solutions:

Most sellers fail miserably at prospecting. The response rate to email is less than 3 percent. The number-one cause: generic, impersonal emails, NOT the value of the solution offered.

I'm reaching out about a tool we've developed (SalesEmail) that automates the personalization of emails through IP data capture. It also runs campaigns with multiple messages and multiple touch points, making prospecting easy for your reps and doubling the average response rates.

Notice the length of the first paragraph. In three short sentences, the message describes the decision maker's point of view—the need to find more prospects, followed by a disruptive truth: emails fail not because of the value of the solution, but because they are generic and impersonal. In the second paragraph, the proprietary solution is narrowed to one. Even though SalesLoft sells a suite of Sales Engagement tools, here I'm only positioning Sales Email. Also, notice that no technical information is shared, just benefits that are easily grasped by the prospect. If you are thinking that more needs to be said, remember that this is just your OCP, not your email or introduction. Your proprietary benefit can be stated or implied but should never include a laundry list of features. The goal here is to provide just enough information for the decision maker to know you offer something unique. When reaching out through those mediums, as we will cover in the next chapter, more should be communicated. Let's look at one more.

Returning to our Braintree example, here's what a completed OCP might look like:

A large percentage of online retailers are losing an important customer segment. Forty-two percent of millennials limit their mobile transactions because of security concerns.

Braintree Control Panel helps you manage the risk and fight next-generation fraudsters. The real-time technology evaluates

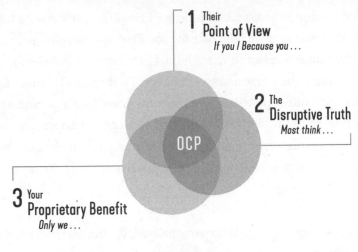

1 Their
Point of View
If you / Because you . . .

2 The
Disruptive Truth
Most think . . .

OCP

3 Your
Proprietary Benefit
Only we . . .

FIGURE 2

hundreds of data points for every transaction to reduce fraudulent transaction attempts, in milliseconds.

Again, the OCP starts with a whiteboard issue—losing an important segment of online customers, followed by a disruptive truth about millennials and, lastly, the proprietary solution—Braintree Control Panel. Unlike in the previous example, there is no proprietary claim. This approach is effective if it's evident to the prospect that you offer something unique.

While the two OCPs above are effective, they are generic. Custom messages always elicit a higher response rate. Thus, for your more qualified prospects, as mentioned earlier in the chapter, talk to an insider, someone who experiences the targeted problem but is not the decision maker. See how some additional information could improve SalesLoft's OCP:

Since the XYZ drug was just approved by FDA and you're adding thirty territory account managers, ensuring they quickly get traction is critical. Most new reps fail miserably at prospecting.

And it's not due to lack of product knowledge; it's due to lack of customer knowledge and how inefficiently they prospect.

We offer a solution that simplifies prospecting. SalesEmail automates the personalization of emails through IP data capture. So your reps will instantly know the CMO's personality profile, relevant business intel, and strategic initiatives. It also automatically creates campaigns with multiple messages and multiple touch points, which can more than double the number of first meetings.

Because this message is so personalized, it can't be ignored. Knowing the drug name, the number of reps, the target audience, and the use of a key metric almost guarantees it will be read. Yes, talking to an insider takes time, but you will be awarded with more appointments.

HOW WELL DOES IT WORK?

You are probably wondering how developing an effective position outperforms the traditional marketing message. We tested, and the short answer is by 366 percent. We identified about 350 qualified prospects to market one of our training solutions (Virtual Selling Skills). We then randomly divided the list into two buckets. Half of the prospects received a well-crafted message about the training solution offered. We were careful to do our best to make the email compelling but not to lead with the prospects' points of view or share a disruptive truth and duplicate what most sellers and marketers do—lead and promote the solution. The other half received an email built around the OCP framework. Thirty-three percent of the recipients who received the OCP email clicked on the link to learn more about the program while the click-through rates from the traditional marketing approach was only 9.09 percent.

Another question I often get is—are all three elements required to get a response? Actually, no. If you are a market leader in the health insurance space and you reach out to the 5 percent of prospects that are currently searching for health insurance, a simple "We offer health insurance" message may work. The purpose of the model is to convert the 95 percent. Your response rate will be proportional to your ability to articulate the prospect's point of view, share a disruptive truth, and offer a proprietary benefit. If the most prevalent problem on the prospect's whiteboard doesn't line up with a proprietary solution, run with it anyway. If you struggle to communicate a disruptive truth, just share a truth. My goal is to provide a framework that will create the highest response rate.

The one recommendation that should never be ignored is to lead with the customer's point of view. Even if you're guessing, being other centered is always more engaging than being self-centered. Also, developing an OCP is difficult. It requires an investment of time and some mental rewiring. If you apply what's offered in this chapter, however, your message will stand out and you will be among the select few to easily engage new prospects.

Another benefit to learning this model is it's the most effective way to present your recommendation. If you learn this framework and process, you will know how to capture the attention of anyone you speak with, enhancing receptivity in any situation. To put this into practice, first focus on one problem or need the customer has that leads to a proprietary benefit and then test it. Once you've spent the time to develop one effective OCP, it becomes easier to build the next.

For additional support in developing your Other-Centered Position, use the template provided online. If you visit the link www.unreceptivebook.com, you will see a useful table for cataloging your list of relevant problems/needs, disruptive truths, and proprietary benefits. Once completed, the hard work is over. Developing an OCP will be effortless.

FIVE

Email and the 10-30-3 Introduction

The typical email, voice mail, or call is getting buried in a tsunami of information. But if you change your approach, you can break through the noise and get more meetings.

We now consume the equivalent of 174 newspapers a day, more than four times the average in the late '80s, and receive anywhere from three thousand to ten thousand messages a day. Not only are we barraged with massive amounts of information, but we are also making more choices with research suggesting an average of 35,000 decisions every day. Think, then, for a moment about the world you are entering when you send an email or make a prospecting call. How many other competitive messages will be sent that day, hour, minute? Where will the recipients receive that email: on their mobile device or computer? Will it be one of the 150 left unread as the decision maker emerges from an all-day meeting, or will it be banished to obscurity as it dies a slow death in the junk folder? To elicit a response, your Other-Centered Position needs to be wrapped in a nice package. Let's start with the most common approach to engaging a new decision maker—email.

THE SUBJECT LINE

Many people make the fatal flaw of minimizing the importance of the subject. On a mobile device, it's about half of the initial message seen by the recipient. It will be the first thing filtered by the RAS to determine if the email is opened. Here's a few typical subject lines from emails I received in the last few months. Do you see any commonalities?

- Introduction to XYZ Company
- A better business communication solution
- Our High-Speed Internet is Faster & More Reliable

Would you read these emails? Do any pique your interest? I deleted them all and actually had to dig them out of my deleted folder to find examples. These could not compete with the other five hundred–plus email messages I received that week. Why? My RAS immediately filtered them out as generic marketing messages, pitches from unknown people who want to sell me something. The bottom line is, zero were about me and none met the RAS criteria.

When crafting your subject line, it's helpful to remember the goal. It's not about getting a meeting or generating a lead. It's about getting noticed. Until the email is read, nothing happens. The goal is to be one of the very few raindrops recognized out of the thousands hitting the windshield—to grab the person's attention without resorting to manipulative tactics that could sabotage your ultimate goal. Here are a few more effective examples and templates to work from:

- [First name], quick question for you
- [Mutual connection] recommended I get in touch
- Ideas for [thing that's important to them]
- Question about [a goal they have, recent event, key initiative]
- Have you considered [thought/recommendation]?

As you develop your subject line, filter it through the following criteria to ensure it gets noticed:

- Does it read like it was sent from someone they know? Or does it appear as if the email was generated by a marketing machine?
- Is the focus of the subject line about your solution or their whiteboard?
- Is it unpredictable? Is the RAS unsure how to file the email?

It's not always possible to pull off all three, but the closer you can get to positively answering the questions above, the higher the response rates. Here are a few real subject lines that worked. Notice how the successful subject lines are less formal and create a mystery that gets the RAS's attention.

SUBJECT
FW: White Flag?
I ignored the first few attempts, but my RAS didn't know what to do with "White Flag." The subject line didn't fit the norm. Also, the FW alerted the RAS that this may be from someone I know. I'm not suggesting you manipulate the customer, just that it was noticed by the RAS and the message got through. In this case, the message had been legitimately forwarded.

SUBJECT
Quick Question About Training Adoption
My number one challenge in effectively delivering our solution and, ultimately, our clients' satisfaction is training adoption. It's one of our top two initiatives at ASLAN. Boom. RAS activated. The subject line not only addressed my whiteboard but appeared to be coming from someone I know without being manipulative or salesy.

FROM   SUBJECT
Delta Airlines   Not Everyone Is Getting This Email

Delta has millions of customers but apparently not everyone got this email. It wasn't the typical canned marketing hype usually received from a large company. This email promised something special for *me*.

SUBJECT
This One Number Proves the Value of a Blog

This got my attention because *I've* struggled to answer the question "Is the effort I put into blogging worth my time?" It's a perceived problem. Plus, I'm curious. What's the one thing? My RAS has to know.

THE EMAIL BODY

To unpack the body of the email, let's work from an example of an email sent by a rep selling voice and data services to an engineering firm with remote employees. (I know, exciting.)

> Subject: Referred by Susan Johnson
>
> Jane,
> I'm reaching out about your twenty-six engineers spread throughout the Southeast. I am currently working with Abbott Engineering Services and Susan suspected you may have the same challenges other engineering firms face while trying to support their remote consultants:
>
> · Wasting time accessing large files on a remote network
> · While at the client site, missing calls from your most strategic customers
> · Hassle dealing with multiple numbers, poor voice quality, and loss of productivity in being disconnected from the main office staff in Atlanta
>
> We just expanded our network and may be able to offer our voice and data services comparable (or possibly less) to what you are paying now. This could ensure your remote employees

have the same support (and voice and data quality) as if they were located at your headquarters in Atlanta.

If this is a priority, let's schedule a brief, fifteen-minute conversation to determine if it makes sense to have one of our engineers offer a free assessment of your current voice and data service.

In the meantime, if you would like to learn more, I've included a case study that highlights the top five problems we solve for virtual, engineering companies (most surprising is the total hours of down time) and how they affect productivity and the bottom line.

Let's deconstruct this email and explore the four sections of an effective email: the connection, the Other-Centered Position, the offer, and the proof. Each are designed to answer the customer's three questions that determine their willingness to engage:

1. Who are you?
2. Can you solve my problem?
3. What's required to move forward?

The Connection: Who are you?

Think about the number one driver behind why you accept an invitation: who's inviting you. We can't overlook that truth when prospecting. You probably don't know the person you are trying to engage. You probably don't have a door-opening name or title. But the fact remains, the more the prospect sees a connection, the higher the probability the email will be read. Therefore, we need to start by providing context for the relationship.

Statistically, emails from people we know are far more read than emails from strangers. An article published by *Fast Company* details the findings of one thousand emails sent to the most difficult audience: executives. What drove the highest response rate? Familiarity. The sender knew something about the recipient, or they leveraged an existing relationship. Another important revelation was that the less generic the message, the higher the response rate. This is why the first sentence of this email works so well.

If you know that the company has "twenty-six engineers spread throughout the Southeast," there must be some connection to Jane. It's the perfect way to make a connection—demonstrate familiarity by focusing on them. Remember, the more specific the details, the higher the click rate. Additionally, referencing Susan and Abbott Engineering (offices in the same office complex) moves the seller from stranger to a "friend of a friend" status. By adding just a few words, you've created an instant connection and interest in knowing more.

If you hadn't talked to Susan and you weren't willing to spend the time calling an insider to capture information, all you would learn from LinkedIn, Google, or their webpage is they have engineers located in the Southeast. Look for something specific you can refer to (for example, hiring in Greenville, layoff, acquiring a new customer, and so on). If you show them a "picture" of themselves, they will always look at it. Always.

THE OTHER-CENTERED POSITION (OCP): CAN YOU SOLVE MY PROBLEM?

Once the connection is made, it's time to deliver your Other-Centered Position. Draw them to your solution by focusing on their whiteboard or point of view, not your solution, a barrier keeping the heroes of the story from getting what they want. As discussed in chapter 4, the customers' point of view will contain three categories of information: (1) what they want, their desired destination, (2) their perspective on how to get what they want, and (3) challenges they face in implementing the plan. Your OCP can start with any of the three, but the one that usually has the most impact is number three. This is where they feel the pain, where confusion exits, and where they have the greatest need. Remember to start with the fire before offering the smoke alarm.

Their Problem

This is where we demonstrate that we know what they're struggling with:

> *You may have the same challenges other engineering firms face while trying to support their remote consultants:*
>
> - *Wasting time accessing large files on a remote network*
> - *While at the client site, missing calls from your most strategic customers*
> - *Hassle dealing with multiple numbers, poor voice quality, and loss of productivity in being disconnected from the main office staff in Atlanta*

The purpose for reaching out is all about Jane, *not* the seller's solution. It describes a perceived need and, because it doesn't lead with a typical sales or marketing pitch, it's unpredictable. Why bullets? With the volume of information being processed on a daily basis, people scan before they read. To draw their attention to what you want them to see, visually serve up the key sound bites in short sentences and bullets. You may spend an hour perfectly crafting your email, but they will delete it in one second if you bury the good stuff.

Disruptive Truth and Proprietary Benefit

This is where we speak to how we can potentially fix the problem:

> *We just expanded our network and may be able to offer our voice and data services comparable (or possibly less) to what you are paying now. This could ensure your remote employees have the same support (and voice and data quality) as if they were located at your headquarters in Atlanta.*

Notice the disruptive truth. The RAS doesn't understand how the remote employees could have the same level of support and quality while operating in the field. At the time of this email, that was unheard of. Next, examine how the seller described the benefit of their proprietary solution. It's better without paying more, and they offer better quality than the competition. Without being manipulative, the best approach is to resist the temptation to provide a detailed, thorough answer but to activate the RAS by creating a little mystery and the need to learn more.

Distill it down to a simple, plausible benefit that the reader wasn't expecting and requires a live conversation to learn more. The goal is to demonstrate the benefit of meeting, not all the features and benefits of your solution. Again, our goal here is for them to believe we *can* fix their problem, not *how* we fix their problem.

Another intriguing benefit is the potential of better service for the same price. This promise could have been met with an eye roll, except for the inclusion of two words: "may be." By dropping the rope, this benefit instantly becomes more believable.

The Offer: What's required to move forward?

Once you've successfully answered the first two questions, it's time to answer the next question: "What's required to move forward?" The answer to this question is always: as little as possible for the customer, while providing the most value.

> If this is a priority, let's schedule a brief, fifteen-minute conversation to determine if it makes sense to have one of our engineers offer a free assessment of your current voice and data service.

The seller drops the rope by simply using the word "If." All assumptions are arrogant, and at this stage, by assuming you know what they should do . . . well, it comes off as arrogant. It's not the message you want to send to a stranger who ultimately needs to trust you enough to give you money.

By communicating you are unaware of their list of priorities and focused on determining what's best for them, it makes you and your email stand out. It's a step toward removing the tension that always exists in the seller-buyer relationship.

Additionally, the offer to only meet for fifteen minutes and introducing the possibility of a free assessment by an engineer reduces the risk to engage and delivers an immediate, cost-free benefit for the buyer. Think baby steps. Again, effective offers remove as many barriers as possible while simultaneously providing the most value to customers. How the email is written will also determine if they perceive the offer has value. By being other centered and dropping the rope, they are much more likely to buy you and therefore your recommendation.

More on "Can You Solve My Problem?"

Most prospects will require more information before accepting your offer. End the email by offering some additional proof to validate your solution:

> In the meantime, if you would like to learn more, I've included a case study that highlights the top five problems we solve for virtual, engineering companies (most surprising is the total hours of down time) and how they affect productivity and the bottom line.

Attach or provide a link that will provide more compelling information on how you have solved this problem for others. Just be sure the information is helpful to addressing the barriers described in the email and demonstrates how you can help them reach *their* desired destination, as opposed to an infomercial on your company or solution. Articles, white papers, and case studies are common, but don't limit your proof to the typical deliverables. Try to come up with some creative alternatives: use Soapbox to create a custom video, share a You-Tube video, send them a book. Remember, unpredictability determines impact. The more you deviate from the norm, the more you stand out.

Lastly, to entice the reader to check out what's to come, be sure to highlight and create a mystery that can be solved only by clicking and/or reading ("most surprising is the total hours of down time").

Our marketing team recently tested this approach by sending a generic email to three hundred recipients. Other than name, there was no attempt to personalize the email. The open rate was 213 percent greater than the industry average, and the click-through rate outpaced the norm by 426 percent. Imagine your success rate if you take a few extra minutes to customize the email.

THE 10-30-3 INTRODUCTION

While email is the most popular channel of reaching out to new prospects, don't overlook the phone. If everyone is using LinkedIn and email, the phone can be a very effective way to reach your prospect. Even if you don't reach decision makers, they will listen to the voice mail. You may not get a call back, but it could lead to a response to one of your other channels of communications, like email.

Research suggests it requires at least six to eight attempts to connect with decision makers. Those stats are based on sending the typical, seller-centric message. But regardless of the number of attempts required, the phone should make it into your rotation of channels for reaching out to new decision makers. It works if you send the right message.

If you are an account manager that can easily walk in the door to meet with existing customers but you need to expand your footprint within the account, engaging new decision makers requires an effective introduction.

Whether face-to-face or over the phone, here's a process that works, in my experience, as much as twenty-two times more effectively than the typical cold introduction. I call it the 10-30-3 introduction. Ten seconds, to get thirty seconds, to get three minutes.

TEN SECONDS

Why do the first ten seconds need special treatment? Unless it's a scheduled meeting, the prospects aren't listening to you. And if you deliver the most important component of your message here, it will be missed.

Your initial goal here is to quiet the voices in their heads: "Who is this? Why are they calling? How did they get my number? Is this a sales call? I have a meeting in five minutes. I answered the phone because I thought it was Nate . . ." In the first few moments, you need to quickly grab their attention but save the best stuff for when they tune in.

There are two keys to quieting the voices. First, reference something that connects you to the individual, either through an existing relationship or something you know about the company or industry. You can always find a connecting point. As we discussed earlier in this chapter about creating an effective email, you need to offer some context for why you are reaching out. Who are you and why did you call?

The second key is to ask a question—a question that will not prematurely end the relationship, such as: "Did River [he's a millennial] tell you I was going to reach out?" "Did you get my email about the work we were doing with your division in California?" If you ask a question about need or desire to engage, such as, "I heard you were interested in . . . ," then one no and you are done.

Yes, you may find the answer to your initial question helpful, but that's not your primary objective. Your goal in the first ten seconds is to get the prospects to say something. By having to answer a question, they are required to focus on the conversation at hand.

A word of caution: if you suspect that a prospect will be extremely closed due to past experience or knowledge of your company, you may need to skip this step. But for most, this approach works and tees you up for the second phase of the introduction—delivering your Other-Centered Position.

THIRTY SECONDS

With their attention, it's time to communicate why it's potentially in their best interest to meet. Here's an example of how a seller who sells health insurance positions their solution:

> *I understand you are covering 100 percent of your thirteen employees' health care costs. With rates expected to rise 22 percent, I thought you may be interested in discussing a plan we created to actually improve your coverage and potentially lower the cost.*

> *If you have a few minutes, I wanted to ask you a couple of questions about your business and then you can decide if it makes sense to set up a meeting to learn more. Do you have two to three minutes to discuss now?*

This is effective because the seller doesn't lead with their solution but begins with the customer's problem: rising health care cost. Then the seller communicates a disruptive truth: improve coverage and potentially lower cost. This not only surprises the prospect but simultaneously insinuates a proprietary benefit.

There's another important element of the second phase of your introduction: drop the rope. Here, more than at any stage of the sales process, we need to eliminate pressure. In the first few seconds of a cold call, receptivity is at the lowest. Words like "may be . . . you can decide" are critical to staying engaged. The prospect isn't closed to a solution but to a sales call. And the more you sound like a seller, the lower your engagement rates will be. In this example, the seller drops the rope four times. It's subtle but sends a clear message that this will be a no-pressure zone. The easier you make it for prospects to say no, the more likely it is they will say yes.

Lastly, I want to highlight the need to ask for permission. Most sellers are uncomfortable with this step for obvious reasons. They've worked so hard to get someone on the phone or to talk with them in the hall. The last thing they want to do is offer to end the call or meeting. If your goal was simply to get the decision maker to talk with you for a few minutes, there is no need to ask permission. But if your goal is a meaningful conversation and to eventually influence their decision, you must have a commitment of time, whether now or in the future.

But the fear of losing the prospect here is valid. This is why you want to lower the risk and avoid asking for anything more than a three-minute meeting. Think baby steps.

THREE MINUTES

Why three minutes? This is the most risk-free step for the decision maker: a three-minute meeting to determine if it makes sense to move onto the next step. Asking for thirty to sixty minutes of a stranger's time is a large mountain to climb. They're struggling to find two hours to spend with their kids, or catch up on rest, or meet deadlines at work. With absolutely zero relational equity, it's a bold request. It's tantamount to a guy asking a stranger out on a date in the first sixty seconds of meeting. It could work, but the chances are slim. It's hard to turn down an other-centered request for a three-minute conversation, and this allows enough time to capture enough information to determine and build value for a more in-depth needs assessment. Because three minutes is so specific, it communicates this is something you've thought about and is therefore legitimate. If you say a few minutes, they will think a minimum of thirty.

Once they agree, you now have the opportunity to ask two or three questions to determine if you can potentially serve the prospect. By understanding a little bit more about their business and key priorities, you can build value in a more in-depth discovery meeting now or in the future.

Twenty-Two Times Better Engagement Rates

Try the 10-30-3 baby step strategy. Ten seconds to get thirty seconds to get three minutes. We tested this in the most hostile cold-calling environment we could possibly imagine: sellers calling people at home about life insurance. I really don't think there is a tougher cold call. Calling a cold prospect at home to secure an appointment with a complete stranger to discuss their impending death is tough stuff.

We observed more than one hundred calls where they connected with more than one hundred prospects. Their standard approach sounded something like this:

> "Mrs. Jones, this is Bob Williams with XYZ Life Insurance. How are you doing today? I'm going to be in your area and wanted to stop by and introduce myself. . . . I would like to just put some information in your hands."

> "Hello, Mr. Smith. This is ____ with _____ Insurance Company. I wanted to offer you an opportunity to see some exciting plans we offer families that include____. I would like to take about fifteen to thirty minutes of your time to go over the plans with you. Do you have any availability next week?"

The results were dismal. The standard approach in the first minute of the relationship is to ask for the decision maker's most precious resource—time. "Hi, I don't know you but I sell this solution that I can't really explain to you now, so I'd like to take two hours of your time to explain it and maybe it'll make sense or maybe not. How about next Tuesday or Thursday?"

When sellers shifted their approach from attempting to set a face-to-face appointment to asking for only a three-minute discovery meeting, their engagement rates (people willing to discuss their needs and determine if a face-to-face meeting was needed) increased from 2.78

percent to 63.64 percent. That's an improvement of twenty-two times. It's hard to believe, but it's true. More importantly, their appointment ratio (number of people willing to meet with sellers in their home after a three-minute meeting) increased from 0 percent to 12.5 percent. The reps that were effective at developing an OCP and followed the 10-30-3 process had a success rate of 20 percent. If it works calling people at home about life insurance, it will work for you.

When the Door Is Open, but the Subject Is Closed

Often when working with existing customers, getting a meeting isn't a challenge, but certain topics are off the table. The conversations are limited to hobbies, family, or what they are currently buying from you. In other words, they are unreceptive to moving beyond how the relationship is defined. They buy XYZ from you, but you know they are unwilling to discuss the ABC they buy from the competition. The door is open, but the subject is closed. Even though they are an existing customer, you still have a receptivity challenge.

The best strategy here is to drop the rope and simply ask permission to discuss. Because of the relational equity, this simple approach will usually lead to a productive conversation. I witnessed this firsthand a few years ago in a sensitive conversation at home. My wife has been chronically ill for twenty years. Following the traditional medical route yielded no relief. We even spent three days at the Mayo Clinic in hopes of finding something that could relieve her pain. It was another dead end and possibly the biggest heartbreak yet. I could see through my wife's tough facade that she was crumbling inside as they explained that she had some type of autoimmune disease and that it was untreatable. They offered her a few alternative options, but it was clear she wasn't receptive. In her mind, she was closing her medical file forever, and it was time to give up hope of recovery. Pursuing additional medical treatment was a subject that was no longer open for debate.

I didn't blame her, but the time came when we were out of options. I'd done my best to play the role of cheerleader, but my heart told me it was time to step into the role of coach. The chosen path had officially hit a dead end, and she needed a medical intervention.

Once the pain from the Mayo trip had eased a bit and the timing was right, I approached the closed subject with a simple question: "Are you open to talking about an alternative approach to treating your illness?" I asked it with as much compassion as I could muster, no judgment and no pressure. I was simply asking permission to put the topic on the table. Should we consider an alternative approach? It was a sincere question, not a recommendation. I made it clear she had freedom to say no, and if she did I would respect that. A gift with strings attached isn't a gift. An invitation where the only acceptable answer is yes isn't an invitation.

She sat back, took a few more bites of her sandwich and said, "I'm not sure. I guess in the past I haven't been. I'll have to think about it."

It was as if she were considering the topic for the first time. All I did was show her the fork in the road, put my arms around her, and support her as she considered the options. I didn't create the options; they always existed, but without standing at the fork she was by default left with only one option—traditional medicine.

Sure, it was tempting to sell her on my preferred recommendation. Her illness affects me as well, albeit not as it does her. But when the choice was offered, without the shove in the back from her husband, she had the freedom to consider what she wanted. That day we began a dialogue where we talked through the pros and cons, including her resistance and fears. The subject shifted from closed to open, and in the end, the alternative path was chosen. Two years later, life has improved dramatically. She did the work and gets all the credit. My role was simply to open a closed subject.

In sales, we often face the same dilemma with our customers. They are closed, not to us but to a specific subject. Those who are successful at opening a closed subject don't dance around the elephant in the room. They plainly ask the customers a simple permission question: "Are you willing to discuss _____?" or "Are you open to _____?" The questions aren't about a customer's willingness to change, they're about receptivity to a conversation. The highest performers in sales put it on the table instead of barging forward, betting that the compelling message will be enough to convert.

To earn a customer's permission to explore new options, a real fear has to be overcome. Namely, there could be an unhappy ending. The customer could say no. That can't and shouldn't stop you from seeking permission to explore. If no is not an acceptable answer, if only your yes path can be chosen, then the potential for receptivity is lost. You are no longer asking for permission—you are assuming permission. The tug-of-war begins.

On the other hand, if a customer's no is acceptable, yes becomes a far more attractive response. The goal is not to trap or manipulate the customers into doing anything. The goal is to simply ask for a low-cost decision: Will they entertain your viewpoint on a previously closed subject? It's your only shot at ensuring an honest dialogue can occur from there forward. And if it does, their receptivity has grown.

As a seller: "We've worked together for a few years now and we've never discussed our solution that could _____. Would you be open to setting up a meeting to talk about it?"

As a parent: "Sweetie, I can tell that you're not jazzed about school. And it's a struggle for you to get your homework done on time. Are you willing to put our heads together and explore ways to make your life easier?"

As a leader: "Based on our last few meetings, I'm sensing you may not be open to coaching. Let's talk about that. Do you want to work together on winning more opportunities or would you rather go it alone? As we talked about, you are responsible for the number, but coaching is optional. My only objective is that you are successful. Maybe someone else can provide better support."

SEVEN

Take the Trip

*The most critical element of converting the Unreceptive is not
how well you articulate your point of view but how well you
validate theirs.*

For more than half a century, Colombia was one of the most violent
and isolated countries on Earth, infamous for cartels, cocaine, and
kidnapping. The Revolutionary Armed Forces of Colombia, or FARC,
fought the government in the longest running war in the Western
Hemisphere—until recently when Colombia achieved what many
thought was impossible. The war is effectively over, the country transformed. How did it happen?

How do you end a fifty-two-year war, which left 220,000 dead and
at least a million displaced, against a revolutionary army dedicated to
overthrowing the government? If you were the president of Colombia, how would you persuade nearly ten thousand guerrilla soldiers
to put down their weapons and come home? Send snipers to kill the
head of the movement? Intensify the military efforts to destroy the
enemy? Attempt to negotiate with the leadership? Juan Manuel Santos
thought differently. He hired an ad executive, Jose Miguel Sokoloff,
who convinced thousands of fighters to give up without firing a shot.
His strategy was simple: he didn't guess what message would persuade the guerrillas to put down their weapons, nor did he attempt

to conjure up his list of benefits for ending the war. He just simply focused on understanding their point of view. He listened, and here's what he learned:

"We found the common denominator of all those stories is that a guerrilla is as much a prisoner of his organization as are the people he holds hostage. There was no way out. And it certainly softened me up when I heard these stories. And I said, 'These poor people.' I didn't expect them to be so human." Even though he was born into the war, for the first time he understood a radically different perspective. They just wanted to come home, but they didn't know how. They were trapped, isolated, with no options. With this new understanding, he launched numerous campaigns: messages from ex-guerillas, Christmas lights on hundreds of trees scattered throughout the jungle, but nothing was more powerful than messages from their mothers asking them to come home. In addition to the recordings, twenty-seven mothers of guerrillas gave photos of their sons and daughters as young children that only they could recognize. During Christmas, flyers with those photos were placed all over the jungle. "The message was: before you were a guerrilla, you were my child. So come home because I will always be waiting for you at Christmastime."

He realized another connection to home was football (that is, American soccer). Football was their passion. So when Colombia hosted the Under-20 World Cup in 2011, Sokoloff kicked off a new campaign. Soldiers armed with thousands of soccer balls entered stadiums, and players, celebrities, and fans all signed them. They loaded them onto helicopters and threw them out over the jungle, each with a sticker that said "Demobilize. Let's play again."

The campaign worked. Juan Manuel Santos won a Nobel Peace Prize for his brilliant strategy to hire an ad executive to peacefully end the war. Why was this so successful at converting possibly the most unreceptive audience—an enemy of war in which both sides experienced heartbreaking tragedy, compounded by a politically polarized ideology? Sokoloff, the brilliant ad executive, understood the listener's point of view.

In the very early days of Apple, Steve Jobs and Steve Wozniak realized they needed two things: corporate expertise and additional capital. It was time to move out of the garage, invest in Apple II, and establish an honest-to-goodness enterprise. Luckily for the founders of Apple, they met Mike Markkula. Mike was an ex-Intel guy who'd made millions in stock options, and they quickly realized he was the one to take them to the next level. The three of them wrote a business plan that included an investment by Markkula of $250,000. For his capital infusion, he now owned a third of the company.

Markkula's plan required Wozniak to quit his engineering job at Hewlett-Packard and join Apple full-time. Markkula made the understandable argument that if he was going to invest in this business, he needed everyone to be 100 percent committed. It seemed like a simple request until they learned that Wozniak was not warm to the idea of leaving HP. Here's an excerpt from the book *Steve Jobs* by Walter Isaacson explaining Wozniak's perspective and how those closest to him tried to change his mind:

> "I felt very insecure in starting a company where I would be expected to push people around and control what they did," Wozniak recalled. "I'd decided long ago that I would never become some authoritative." . . . But Jobs got very upset. He cajoled Wozniak; he got friends to try to convince him; he cried, yelled, and threw a couple of fits. He even went to Wozniak's parents' house, burst into tears, and asked Jerry (the father) for help. By this point Wozniak's father had realized there was real money to be made by capitalizing on the Apple II, and he joined forces on Jobs' behalf. "I started getting phone calls at work and home from my dad, my mom, my brother, and various friends," Wozniak recalled. "Every one of them told me I'd made the wrong decision." None of that worked.

Wozniak explains how a meeting with Allen Baum, a high school classmate, changed everything. Baum understood Wozniak's point of view and pointed out that he would not have to go into management or give up being an engineer. "That was exactly what I needed to hear," Wozniak later said. "I could stay at the bottom of the organizational chart, as an engineer." He called Jobs and declared that he was now ready to come on board.

It's not hard to imagine the position that Jobs, Wozniak's father, and all the other close friends took in attempting to influence Wozniak. I'm sure it had to do with money, power, success, control, living the dream, or any number of reasons that all made perfect sense to them. Only Baum saw what was truly important to Wozniak. Access to Wozniak wasn't the challenge. The door was open, but the subject was closed. What was different about Baum's approach? He understood a critical principle to influencing the Unreceptive.

THE POLAR PRINCIPLE

Imagine you are standing on the North Pole and the person you are trying to influence is standing on the South Pole (see Figure 3). What would "up" and "down" be for the person on the North Pole? The South Pole? Because of your vantage point, your perception of "up" is very different. In fact, it's the exact opposite. Now, imagine attempting to convince someone to change their definition of "up."

FIGURE 3

Steve Jobs's "up" was about building a great company, designing innovative products, and being in control of his and his company's destiny. From Wozniak's perspective, however, joining Apple full-time meant losing his role as an engineer. His "up" meant working in a secure company, void of managerial responsibility. Because of who they were and how they saw the world, they had polar opposite points of view. Views they would, and did, vehemently defend.

You face the same dilemma every day. Your goal is to get someone to change, and you have valid reasons why this change is good. It's how you see the world; it's your "up." But you, like all of us, constantly encounter people who don't want to change. The door is open, but the subject is closed. "I'm not leaving HP" . . . "I'm happy with the current solution" . . . "I don't have a drinking problem." In your mind, you see it clearly and they are just wrong. "But, up is up!" you say.

How do you get others to see your point of view? Some will tell you to meet them halfway. The flaw in that strategy is that you are the one with the goal to influence them. They are convinced nothing needs to change. Asking for them to make an investment to meet in the middle is often futile. Plus, when meeting in the middle, "up" is confusing to both parties. No, the first step in tilling the soil is to take the trip, the whole trip. By validating others' perspectives, you not only greatly increase the odds they will listen to your recommendation, but you also gain important intel. But here's probably the most compelling reason to take the trip: it's hypocritical to expect customers to be receptive to your point of view if you are not receptive to theirs.

VALIDATE THEIR POINT OF VIEW

We have to lay aside our agenda and see the world through their vantage point. The Polar Principle reveals why. We are unreceptive to an opposing point of view until we feel our position is heard, understood, and validated.

A few years ago, Dan, the account manager for a Fortune 500 tool manufacturer, was running their typical route. Seven forty-five-minute presentations on the latest tools to large electrical distributors. You "unload, show, and go" as they like to say. At the beginning of his third meeting, he sensed a receptivity problem. The owner stood stoically, arms folded, like a teenager hearing a lecture on the consequences of social media. Instead of ignoring the elephant in the room, Dan decided to take the trip. He paused long enough to get the owner's attention, looked him in the eye, and said: "I can't help but notice it looks like you're not too excited to be here."

"You tool guys are all the same," said the owner. "You show up, make your pitch, pack up, and leave."

Dan wisely stopped his demo and asked, "Sounds like you've had some problems?"

"Yes, I have! In fact, I've got a tool right now that doesn't work."

"That's not good. I can see why you feel that way. Let's have a look."

They walked over and discovered that the defective tool was the competitor's. This didn't deter the seasoned sales guy; he fixed the tool. It didn't matter who made it; he would fix it. Now the customer was more open, and a productive conversation began about the owner's business and how Dan could offer more value. The meeting ended with an order for a brand-new line of high-end drill bits. The outcome of the meeting radically changed not because Dan knew how to sell tools but because he took the trip. Once he got off his demo soapbox and tuned into the customer's point of view, influence began. What did Dan understand? When there are polarized points of view, customers will never embrace your perspective until you validate theirs.

Every time we enter into a situation in which we want to influence, there are always two points of view—yours and theirs. The life they have lived and their set of experiences are always different from yours. You have to make an effort to understand their set of experiences.

AS RODNEY DANGERFIELD SAID, "TOUGH CROWD"

Think about your most difficult presentation, your toughest audience, or the time when you had little to no shot at changing the minds of the decision-making team. But, despite the odds, you showed up anyway. Got it? You remember the day? I promise you it doesn't come close to the audience Erin Gruwell faced in the early fall of 1994.

In your scenario, the decision-making team probably didn't vehemently hate you or want you dead. That's literally the receptivity of the audience Erin faced in her first teaching job at Woodrow Wilson High School, a tough Los Angeles–area school district. Her assignment: teach English to the worst performing students of the sophomore class. How would you reach these kids? How would you get them interested in literature or English composition? What would be the first few slides of your PowerPoint presentation?

They didn't care about an education. They cared about staying alive. As one of her students put it, "I never thought I would graduate. If I have to do a book report and worry about being shot, like the book report is going to be at the bottom of my priority list." She intuitively knew if she was going to reach them, she had to learn more about her students. But how? Relationally, there was a huge chasm. She was a self-described perky, upper-middle-class woman who wore polka dots. They were tough street kids who watched their friends die weekly.

While our role in sales is clearly different from Erin's, there is one common challenge: How do you change strongly held beliefs? Not take orders or manage relationships but change beliefs. Erin had to change her students' beliefs about the best path to reach their desired destination, a path they viewed with the utmost skepticism. Sound familiar? She pulled it off. She was so successful, her story became a movie, *Freedom Writers*, starring Hilary Swank. She revolutionized the way they viewed education, and 100 percent of her 150 students graduated from high school.

The first of Erin's many brilliant ideas was to push her agenda aside. Instead of diving into diagramming sentences or the merits of iambic pentameter, she made one simple, other-centered request: journal your thoughts for two weeks. Since the journals were turned in anonymously, she got the real story for the first time. Her students became people. She got a glimpse into the way they saw the world, what their life was really like, and the incredible challenges they faced every day. She discovered their point of view. She gained valuable intelligence.

I believe Erin, like all the other teachers before her, would have failed to influence her students if she hadn't begun with their story and desired to find out more about them. So simple but, in my experience, so overlooked. Her students, like your customers, have an existing frame for how they see the world. Everything they've experienced in life determines how they see the topic at hand. And if you desire to reframe a strongly held belief system, you must find out what the existing frame is. This isn't just intel gathering for the sake of it. It is to help you genuinely connect, determine what's relevant, and find empathy for the person you're trying to influence.

As explored in chapter 3, our greatest needs are love, acceptance, and worth. Taking the trip is our greatest opportunity to meet that need. When we choose to set our agenda aside and make the other person the central figure in the story, they feel chosen and valued. This enhanced emotional connection may have more impact on your success than the information.

Not only will you know exactly how to position your solution, you have the opportunity to develop a unique message and greatly increase the chances that the other person will reciprocate, take the trip, and see your point of view as well. Someone has to struggle. Either they must struggle to understand our point of view or we struggle and take the trip to understand their point of view. As sellers, we must go first. We make the decision to struggle to understand what may seem like an insane viewpoint until we set aside our point of view and make the journey.

You walk into a sales meeting, confident that what you are about to deliver will hit the mark. You quickly realize the customer has a much different perspective. Take the trip.

You land the meeting you've been pursuing for six months. The decision maker communicates a strong interest in your solution. Then, at the meeting, a new player takes a seat and leads the conversation in a different direction, the wrong direction. You are naturally frustrated that another roadblock has surfaced. Take the trip.

You've been advised by key players to deliver your presentation to the senior vice president. You've rehearsed countless times, confirmed the meeting objective, and asked all the right questions. Within the first five minutes, the SVP strongly communicates that your presentation is missing the mark; she's looking for something different. Take the trip.

You are having lunch with a close friend when you are blindsided by an accusation that you believe is completely unwarranted and, frankly, ridiculous. You're wounded and stunned. Take the trip nonetheless.

What if they are emotional? Take the trip.

What if they are wrong? Take the trip.

There is never a scenario where taking the trip first doesn't lead to higher receptivity and ultimately a better outcome. There may be a scenario in which you don't have the opportunity to take a deeper dive into the mind of the listener, like if you were speaking to a room full of people or making a presentation to a committee of decision makers when a discovery meeting isn't possible. This is a reality we all sometimes face as sellers. Here, the challenge is more daunting, but the need remains.

Sometimes taking the trip will be captured through research about your audience. Other times, taking the trip will be a one-on-one meeting where you have the opportunity to interview the person you desire to influence. Regardless of the situation or your level of access, your objective is to let go of your own agenda so that you can have an "oh" moment.

THE "OH" MOMENT

How do you know when you've reached your destination, when the trip is complete? You will have a moment of clarity when you understand why they feel what they feel or believe what they believe. It will come to you in an "Oh, *now* I see why you feel that way" moment. This is when your confusion, and maybe even frustration, is replaced with empathy. This is the spark that ignites your ability to influence.

Erin Gruwell was humble enough to see her students' perspective, and it radically altered her approach. Much like a friend of mine who teaches math in one of the most poverty-stricken areas of Atlanta. He recently shared this heartbreaking story: "I was really struggling to connect with one of my seventeen-year-old students. She was completely checked out. Nothing I did or said got through. I couldn't reach her. So I decided to drive to her home and see if I could get a clearer picture of what was causing her to check out. I soon discovered that her sister was raped in her home and her mother was a crack dealer. At night, she was working at Kroger to feed the family. I quickly realized, I was looking into the teeth of a hungry animal just trying to survive." *Oh!* He literally took a trip and genuinely, compassionately validated the barriers she faced. Once that occurred, a relationship emerged, receptivity began to blossom, and he was able to influence her decision about the importance of getting an education.

When another person's point of view doesn't make sense, remember there is something you don't understand. There is something that, if you knew it, your confusion would disappear. The first step to influencing other people's beliefs is to resolve your confusion, not attempt to change their perspective. Once we have that breakthrough moment, we can validate their point of view and hear the magic word: *exactly*.

"EXACTLY"

Listeners don't feel that their deep emotional needs are uniquely understood until you feed it back to them. When taking the trip, your ultimate goal is to articulate the customer's point of view as well or better than they can. If you do, you will hear a word that signals an opportunity to influence: *exactly*. Not only will this response confirm that you understand, but you will also sense a positive shift in the listener's emotional state. The soil begins to loosen. In that instant, resistance falls and receptivity skyrockets.

It's important to remember that understanding doesn't equal agreement. Leaving your agenda behind to understand someone else's point of view doesn't mean your recommendation is permanently tossed aside. Your goal is to understand why they believe what they believe. You honor them by respecting and validating their point of view. Their point of view doesn't change the truth; it just opens the door to having a meaningful conversation about the truth.

ESTABLISHING CREDIBILITY

There's another payoff for demonstrating you understand and accept the listener's point of view: credibility is established. This is another area in which our intuition sabotages our success. Most of us believe that credibility is established by demonstrating our knowledge and expertise on a particular subject. While that certainly plays a part, the truth is that demonstrating we understand their problem pays the highest dividends.

I learned this early in my sales career. I would consistently win deals against reps who clearly had more expertise. How? Because of this truth: the decision maker believes the person who best understands the problem is the most qualified to solve the problem. Even though this is not always the case, it's the ancillary benefit of taking the trip. Even if our recommended solution will ultimately yield the highest return on investment, we can lose the competitive advantage to a lesser qualified solution. If they "get it" and you don't, you are perceived as less qualified. How many times have you scratched your head after losing a deal? "How did I lose to those guys?" It's often because of the flawed belief that it's more important to tell others what I know than demonstrate I understand their unique world.

I'm often asked, "How is this different from the traditional discovery process?" The focus of a typical discovery meeting is to lead the listener to our recommendation. A set of questions has been created to uncover a need for the solution we sell. In contrast, taking the trip is about moving away from our solution and understanding the heart and mind of the listener. To be effective, we drop the rope, set our solution aside, leave the North Pole, and search for what it feels like to be the listeners and why they believe what they believe. We have to let go of our desire to pull them to our point of view in order to take the trip.

BARRIERS TO TAKING THE TRIP

Over the years of teaching sellers how to take the trip, I have noticed two common barriers. They are both thoughts people have that get in the way of being curious about the other's viewpoint. One is a flaw in strategy, and one is related to fear. Let's start with the easy one first.

Barrier One: "I know what they are going to say."

Let's just assume this is true. You know everything about those customers or prospects you are meeting with. You know the informal drivers of their decisions, even the ones they struggle to articulate. You know intimate details about their resources, priorities, wants, needs, existing relationships, and strongly held biases. That may all be true, but here is why you still need to endeavor to take the trip and validate their point of view. The information you gain by taking the trip is secondary to the emotional connection and receptivity that occurs when you set aside your agenda, your beautifully crafted pitch, and validate their point of view. Remember that their willingness to listen is always more important than your ability to communicate.

When was the last time you met with someone and the person's only agenda was to understand your point of view? The person listened, validated everything you said, and wasn't just waiting for a turn to talk. It's probably been a minute. How did you feel about this unicorn of a situation? Were you more or less likely to listen?

Let them go first. Tune in and demonstrate that he or she is the most important person on the planet. Remember the LAW that drives all relationships and describes the customer's greatest need: love, acceptance, and worth. Meeting this emotional need is far more important than the thing you are so excited to sell.

It's very common for experienced sellers to struggle with this barrier. Because they really have heard it all. All the stories start sounding the same. You really could finish most customers' sentences: "You're a family of six, with young children, you want a minivan with good gas mileage." Slow down and remember taking the trip isn't just about information, it's about demonstrating how much you value other human beings. Be sincerely more interested in them than the story they tell, and when the time comes to influence, they will listen to you.

Barrier Two: "I won't know how to respond to the information shared."

If taking the trip is new for you, or you are new in your role, this fear is justified. You know that as long you stick with your talking points, recite your memorized billboards, you are in your comfort zone. Just stick to the script of the guided tour. You may be less effective, but at least you don't feel like a middle-aged adult learning the latest TikTok dance.

Let me challenge you with a truth that helped me overcome some of my greatest fears. If you are going to succeed at anything, you must be willing to fail. Unless you are a trust fund kid, avoiding failure is not an option. If you stay in your comfort zone, you will be the same person, with the same abilities, twenty years from now. That should terrify you. I love how Lionel Richie explained this truth to an *American Idol* contestant, "Life begins at the end of your comfort zone."

Our family went on our first ski trip when I was nine years old. My mom was twenty-nine (they start young in Tennessee). We both fell in love with skiing that year. Every year after, my dad always found a way to take us skiing again, even the lean years. Mom and I were both progressing nicely in our skills. And then one day my mom fell and broke her leg in two places. It changed everything. Even though she continued to ski and was a talented athlete, she never got off the bunny slopes. She skied well into her sixties but never improved beyond the day she broke her leg in Crested Butte. By age sixteen, I was able to tackle almost any slope on the mountain. Why the two different outcomes? She was still young and had plenty of time to recover. After the break, she was simply afraid to fall again.

Be willing to fall. If you don't know what to do with the information revealed by customers, say you will get back with them. If you ask a few awkward questions, work on making them better. In a few months, you will know more than most sellers who've been in the business for twenty years. This is why every year fewer and fewer customers are interested in working with sellers when evaluating solutions. They believe reps are just talking websites. To offer value beyond what's available on the internet, get to know your customers and how they see the world, not just the data needed to position your solution. Because of the collected knowledge gained from hundreds of conversations, you will soon be in the enviable position of knowing more than the people you meet with. You quickly move from the bunny slopes to skiing the black diamonds.

EIGHT

The Discovery Roadmap

If you're taking a trip you've never been on before, you need a roadmap. This is the most overlooked tool in selling—developing an effective framework for guiding discovery.

Most sellers have questions, but they are rarely clear about their discovery objectives. They wing it and get lost. Taking the trip requires a roadmap and the ability to drive. In the next chapter, I will explore the necessary skills for leading a successful discovery meeting (that is, how to drive). But first, let's examine the tool that guides you toward your destination.

Although a discovery framework is a very conventional sales tool, it does affect the emotional receptivity of your customer or prospect. Without a roadmap, it's difficult to lead the discovery process fluently and confidently. Our lack of competency in this area can erode the decision maker's willingness to reveal crucial information.

To build a roadmap, once again we start by focusing on the customer or prospect's point of view. When prospecting, we do our best, based on our experience or inside information, to guess the customer's point of view in order to answer the question "Why meet?" (that is, your Other-Centered Position). In discovery, we stop guessing and seek to understand others' points of view. Once you have clarity on the problems that inhibit them from getting what they want and their perspective on how they want to solve it, you will have the information to determine your other-centered recommendation. Simply put, to build a roadmap, you need to answer these three questions:

1. Is there a problem you can and should solve?
2. What's the customer's perspective on the best way to solve the problem?
3. What's the best way to solve that problem—regardless of what you sell?

The first two questions are answered by learning the customer's point of view. This is where discovery begins and where our roadmap starts. Nothing you will do during the sales process will have a greater impact on receptivity than understanding, caring about, and validating the customer's point of view. This is how you learn how decisions are made. If you miss this, you will either be chasing an unqualified opportunity and/or lack the ability to effectively position your solution.

Next, our focus will shift from discovering what customers want to determining what they really need. Here is where you establish your value to decision makers. By having the expertise to help the customer determine the best solution, you are embraced as a partner, not a sales rep. You earn a seat at the decision-making table while other product pushers make follow-up calls to touch base, check in, and see how things are progressing.

Offering a comprehensive and generic roadmap for all sellers isn't possible. Believe me, I've tried. What follows are the broad categories to guide you in developing your framework. This is by no means designed to be a comprehensive roadmap.

POINT OF VIEW: DISCOVER THE PROBLEM

In discovery, the questions are less important than the information you seek. Therefore, the first step in building a roadmap is to define your objectives. To determine if a relevant problem exists, you have three objectives: the decision maker's desired destination, problems or barriers to reaching that destination, and the impact of solving the problem. The payoff for solving the problem determines the willingness to invest the time and money in a solution to the problem.

So your first goal is to determine what the decision maker wants. Resist the temptation to ask questions that lead to your solution, but focus on how their performance will be evaluated at the end of the year. Your ultimate goal is to determine if your solution is required to reach their destination. Does their success hinge on buying your product, service, or solution?

Regardless of what type of decision makers you are working with, from consumers to executives, they want something. You start here because their desired destination is nonnegotiable and is what they are most passionate about. If you fail to uncover something they want and a problem (known or unknown) in getting what they want that you can address, you have no solution to offer. But if a problem is discovered, it's time to move to the second component of customers' points of view: their perspective.

POINT OF VIEW: DISCOVER THEIR PERSPECTIVE

Your objectives here are threefold, as well. What's the customer's perspective on:

1. How the problem should be fixed;
2. Who should fix it; and
3. If an external solution is needed (that is, the problem can't be solved with existing resources), what are the criteria for determining the best external solution?

Since the first two are fairly straightforward, let's take a closer look at number three. Accurately uncovering the decision criteria for choosing a solution and a solution provider is a challenge for all sellers.

Rarely, if ever, do we have time to communicate all key aspects of our solution. Like a movie director determining what ends up on the cutting room floor, we must choose what to cut from our presentation. If you are an experienced seller, you know the importance of determining and prioritizing what drives customers' decisions and using that knowledge to determine the content of your presentation. But what if you are wrong? Is it possible to ask all the right questions and still miss the critical drivers behind their decision? Yes. Because all too often, they struggle to articulate what they really care about. Like describing their dream house to an architect, sometimes they just don't know what they care about until they see it. In sales, waiting for that reaction is usually too late. The bottom line is you can't rely on decision makers to accurately communicate their decision criteria. Are they being deceitful? In my experience, no. They just struggle to quantify what's most important to them and they need our help.

Consider how you choose lodging for a vacation. It seems simple enough, but it often becomes more complicated than it appears. Imagine you had to delegate the planning of your summer vacation to one of your best friends. How would you instruct your friend to select the perfect hotel? Is it a matter of price? Location? Food? Ambience? Service? Do you care more about the room or where you will hang out in the hotel?

"Well, it depends," you say. It depends on whether the kids are going. It depends on what's near the hotel. It depends on budget, and so on. There are so many options, and this plethora of options is why so many of us hate to plan a trip. We're not sure how to make the best decision, and due to our uncertainty, many of us procrastinate or just play it safe and go with a brand of hotel that has the best reputation. "I'm sure they have it figured out," we say. "I just don't have the time to figure out all my options." And this is why many of us who are in business lose to the number one player in our space. They are the most well known and therefore the safe option.

Now step into the world of a decision maker. Not only are there a lot of variables, there are other dynamics in play. If they make the wrong decision, the consequences are huge. They could lose political capital, lose incentives, or even get fired. The point is, they may need your help to determine their preferences. To help them cull through and rank their criteria, think about the last time you got your eyes checked. The doctor offers a simple technique for focusing on (see what I did there) the most important criteria.

THE EYE TEST

When checking your eyesight, the optometrist asks us to choose between only two options: "Can you see this red barn . . . or not? Is lens A better or is lens B better?" When narrowed down to one choice, it's much easier to decide which we prefer. Use this approach to aid you and the decision makers in prioritizing the decision criteria.

Once you've discovered their list of criteria (for example, cost, experience, customized service), pick two and ask them to choose which is the most important. If you continue this process, the top criteria will be crystal clear.

Benefit A or Benefit B?

Global capabilities or quality of service?

Industry experience or custom solution?

They may struggle to answer, but the dialogue will yield important insight into what is most important to them. Here's some additional tips on discovering the crucial decision drivers:

- Know all the possible decision drivers in advance. If you know all the possibilities, it's easy to look at the list and determine if you or the decision maker have overlooked important criteria.
- To shift from a cost discussion, remove price from the list. Start by asking the question "Other than price, how will you make a decision to choose one company/solution over another?"

- Hidden and often more important drivers are revealed by the decision makers' questions and their reaction to what you say. Pay attention to what they seem most interested in or concerned about. Additionally, ask about how past decisions were made when buying a similar solution. This may tip you off to decision criteria that will never show up in a written document.

- What's important to the one evaluating the solution may not be the same as the one who ultimately makes the decision. Determining the decision maker and the decision-making team is a complex topic for another book, but it's important to remember if you're applying this book's principles to influence the wrong people, it will fail to get the results you seek.

DETERMINE YOUR RECOMMENDATION
AND PROPRIETARY BENEFITS

Decision makers' perspectives on the solution needed don't always provide the best way to solve their problem. With an other-centered motive, you shift roles from understanding what they want to determining what they need, from journalist to consultant.

Based on the collective knowledge of you and others in the organization, you play the role of a free consultant and gain the information you need to determine if there is a better path to the desired destination. Those sellers who are effective at quickly assessing the situation have clearly defined the data points needed to determine their other-centered recommendation. I witnessed a simple but effective example of this while watching a recent rerun of the '90s sitcom *Seinfeld*.

Two of the main characters, Kramer and George, were meeting at their usual hang spot, the corner diner. Kramer had an agenda: convince George to move to California. Kramer auditioned for a movie, got the acting bug, decided to move to LA, and wanted George to join him. But when Kramer floated the idea, George vehemently resisted: "I love my life in New York." Subject closed. Kramer was faced with an unreceptive audience who was blind to a few pitfalls related to his seemingly perfect life in New York.

How would you try to convince someone to move to California? Focus on the benefits of the weather, the lifestyle, and so on? Develop a SWOT (strengths, weaknesses, opportunities, and threats) analysis on LA vs. NYC? Kramer tried a different tactic that bolstered receptivity and radically affected George's view of his life in New York. We pick up the scene in which George is passionately stating his life in New York is perfect and therefore there is no reason to move.

"I'm not wasting my life (in New York). I am *living* my life," he proclaimed, pounding the table. Kramer didn't have a rebuttal. He just calmly leaned across the table and began asking a few questions as if to honestly explore whether or not George should reconsider.

"Do you have a job?"

"No."

"Do you have any prospects?"

"Ah . . . no." George softens.

"Do you have a woman?"

"No."

Kramer continues, "Do you have any prospects?"

"No."

"Do you have any money?"

"Ah . . . no." George now sounds a bit depressed.

"Do you have reason for even getting up in the morning?"

"I like to get the *Daily News*," George says as if on the verge of tears.

As George began to answer those questions, "no" . . . "no" . . . "no" . . . "no," his demeanor and point of view changed. He went from passionately defending his position that his life was amazing to "I have a huge problem." Kramer's questions helped George discover an unknown problem. Five minutes before the conversation, George's plan for his life seemed plausible. Now, he's not so sure.

This silly example nicely points out why Kramer's approach worked and so many sellers fail to determine if there is a flaw in the decision maker's plan. Kramer had a clear understanding of what information was needed to help George see an unknown problem: job, woman, purpose, and money.

Let's apply this to your world. Regardless of the decision maker's point of view, have you, like Kramer, identified the categories of information to determine the best solution? The information doesn't necessarily lead to your solution but to the right solution. The best solution may be to maintain the status quo, utilize internal resources, delay, or a partial version of what you would like to sell. To help you compile your categories, ask yourself:

- When implementing this solution, what are the best practices identified by working with previous customers that are required for success? Stated another way, what must happen to ensure the customer realizes the payoff? Identifying these categories may not change or affect the solution you offer.
- What is typically overlooked by your customers? If they haven't been down this road before, where have others made a wrong turn?
- What do you need to know about their business and needs to assess the situation and make a recommendation?

When you have a clear understanding of how to assess their situation and expose hidden pitfalls in the plan, you send a clear message to decision makers: you have expertise they lack and provide value well beyond the solution you sell. Simply put, it positions you as a trusted partner.

You move from sales rep to being part of the decision-making team. But without a fluid understanding of those pitfalls, the trip may end. You ask if they want to "move to LA" and they respond with "no, my life is great here in New York"; how do you respond? You are left with overcoming an objection with little knowledge. Receptivity diminishes or disappears as you sell the merits of "LA" without honestly determining what's best for them.

Conversely, when you understand and lead the customer through a process in which together you thoroughly examine the best path forward, you instantly differentiate yourself from other reps just pitching a solution. The decision maker sees you as a critical resource versus a rep who just sells things.

Once you've completed the process and determined your recommended solution, identify the aspects of that solution that are proprietary by asking four questions:

- What are the features and benefits of the relevant products and services that no one else can offer?
- Are there ways you develop, deliver, maintain, or support the solution that differentiates you from the competition?
- Can you leverage the company's resources to create a unique solution for the customer that can't be duplicated? This doesn't require changing a product or service but is achieved by how you creatively customize your solution.
- What can I do to outwork the competition and leverage my expertise to ensure the decision maker sees me as a valuable part of the solution? Remember you should always be the proprietary component of your solution.

This information is critical when building value and demonstrating why to choose you over all the other options. But before blindly moving to the next step or investing more resources, take time to soberly assess your probability to win. Your chances are directly proportional to how much of the needed solution is uniquely offered by you. A key component of being other centered is choosing well. So here we step back, take an unbiased look at their needs, and if you're not set up to serve them well, move on. If you were an orthopedic surgeon that focused on knees and shoulders, how would you serve a patient who complained of knee pain but discovered during the examination that the problem was actually due to a back problem? You'd send them somewhere else and move onto the next patient.

To help you in your development of your roadmap and time-tested questions in determining the formal and informal decision drivers, visit www.unreceptivebook.com to access templates and additional discovery resources.

NINE

How to Get Anyone to Tell You Anything

You can't change a closely held belief if you don't know what that belief is. To influence, you need to discover the unfiltered truth.

To influence and to sell, you need the truth about what people want, what they fear, who is driving the decision, and how the decision will be made. To differentiate your solution, you must know the decision drivers. I'm not talking about the published list that appears on a spreadsheet. All the contenders get access to that list. I'm talking about the informal stuff—the two or three desires or concerns the decision maker rarely utters, if ever at all.

"I'm not really the decision maker. Even though I'm the VP, Kinsey knows much more about this than I do."

"I need to really trust you to manage this project. I have a sick child at home."

"I need a lot of support. I'm not really sure I know what I'm doing."

"Everyone likes the firm we've been working with. You will have to do something amazing to move us away from____."

"I don't really believe ____ can do that. I've tried it before."

When receptivity is low, the truth is harder to discover (see Figure 4). Like conducting a survey at the mall, you are offered one- or two-word answers, the surface level information offered to strangers. To paraphrase Tom Cruise in *A Few Good Men*, "You want the truth!"

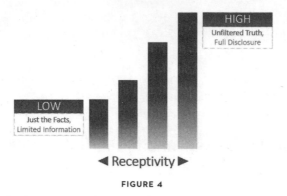

FIGURE 4

Discovering the truth and motivating the customer to move from just revealing the facts to full disclosure of wants, fears, desires, and needs hinges on two critical skills: how you ask questions and how you respond to what the customer has to share. Since discovery begins with questions, let's start there.

THE PRINCIPLE OF THE DARK

Have you ever been in the back of a taxi when the driver took a different route from the one you expected? What did you assume? Did you think to yourself, "He's obviously discovered a shortcut or there must be an accident on Highway 95. That driver is really taking care of me!" Was that your thought? Probably not. No, we assume they are jacking up the fare.

Why? Because of what I call the Principle of the Dark: *When prospects or customers are in the dark about your motive or your ability to help, they assume a negative.* In the bestselling book *Crucial Confrontations*, the authors explain it this way: "We see (or hear) what that person did and then tell ourselves a story about why he or she did it, which leads to a feeling which leads to an action." Because of how listeners perceive our role, the story they tell themselves when they see and hear something questionable is almost always negative. Decades of studies were cited that showed people default to attributing a negative motive when asked to judge a person's behavior, be they seller or not.

This can be seen in our personal relationships. Think about the last time a friend was late for lunch. Did you attribute a positive motive? Did you assume he was in trouble or that he was selfish or undisciplined? If a colleague doesn't return your email or text, do you typically assume she's overwhelmed at work? Or did you feel a bit ignored, assuming that you're just not that important? Every argument I ever had with my wife can be traced back to perception of motive.

I recently heard the story of an executive traveling to a regional office to provide direction to the troops. As he was talking to the team about some critical changes in the company, he noticed someone typing on their phone. Or at least that's what he assumed. What would you assume? Annoyed, the executive called the person out for texting during the meeting. He later learned the employee was taking notes to be sent to other team members unable to attend the meeting . . . *as his manager had asked him to do*. Oops. Principle of the Dark in action.

The decision maker *will* jump to conclusions. It's unavoidable. We just need to turn on the lights. We need to think through how we ask and position questionable questions.

POSITIONING QUESTIONABLE QUESTIONS

The purpose of some questions is obvious:

"What's your strategic plan for X?"

"What challenges are you facing with Y?"

These types of questions are clearly about the decision maker and relate to the perceived reason for meeting. But the motive behind some questions you pose is not so obvious, such as:

"What's your budget?"

To which your client may assume: "They are trying to figure out how much I can spend. The cost will magically be whatever I tell them my budget is."

Or: "Who else is involved in the decision-making process?"

"Of course they want to know that," your client may think. "They don't want to lose a deal. They will try and go around me. Do they think I'm not capable of handling this?"

Of course, decision makers wouldn't probably admit to having these thoughts, but ask yourself why they don't reveal the complete story. Why does discovery sometimes stall? Either the listeners aren't interested in the subject matter or they don't trust your motive. By effectively positioning your questions, you can address both—make the question about them and for them.

Questions about budget, current relationships, the decision-making process, or any subject for which your motive is unclear, or the information revealed, could backfire and need to be primed with an other-centered purpose.

"Let's talk about your budget. Do you have a budget in place? The reason I'm asking is we have several options for how we could potentially work with you. I want to recommend a solution that's in line with what you are looking for."

"I'm sure you are considering a few of our competitors. Do you mind sharing who else will be making a presentation? Knowing this will help me point out what is unique about our solution and ultimately help you make the best decision. Since we will only have about an hour, I want to make sure we focus on what is most important to you."

If you're struggling to rephrase a "questionable question," this shines a spotlight on your true intent. The information you seek serves *you* but not the customer—which is not necessarily a bad thing. You want to win, but if you want a more productive dialogue, the customer needs to be consistently reminded that you are passionate about protecting their win, as well.

We naturally default to self and therefore what comes naturally is what *we* want—whether in discovery or any stage of the sales process. It's like teaching a kid to eat candy—unnecessary. This is why top sellers spend less time on the questions *they* want to ask and focus more on *why* the customer should reveal sensitive information.

"The Reason I'm Asking Is . . ."

Here's another benefit to learning to effectively position your questions: it eliminates your fear. When you are confident that the tough questions you need to ask will help the customer, it frees you up to move into subjects you've previously avoided. Potential conflict or the erosion of trust will be avoided if you can say, "The reason I'm asking is . . ." These five magic words have the power to position you as a partner, not the typical seller. Will this always work? No. As we unpack throughout this chapter, there's definitely more to getting the customer to reveal the unfiltered truth; but the first step is removing doubt about your motive. Your motive may be pure, but the decision maker has one more question before they are willing to tell the whole story: "Am I wasting my time?"

Attach a Disruptive Truth

None of us like wasting time divulging information to someone who can't solve the problem. There's no reason to provide a detailed explanation to your neighbor about an engine problem if he or she is not a mechanic. Studies have revealed that only 13 percent of customers believe sellers can understand their needs. The keyword is *can*. This reveals how customers and prospects enter into the selling process, skeptical that what they need to share will be understood. The deck is stacked against you.

That's why, as a general rule, most decision makers don't meet with sales reps. They delegate the information gathering to an evaluator to determine what solution is needed. Why? Because the decision maker believes that most sales reps are just, well . . . a rep. He or she isn't a consultant but a representative of a company or solution. In decision makers' minds, a rep certainly can't tell them something that they don't already know about the problem they face. Again, this perception is not rooted in the truth about you, but it exists nonetheless.

You may have the expertise to run their company, but decision makers' investment in discovery is guided by their assumption about you, not the truth about you. So, assuming you do have valuable expertise to offer, how do you convince them that you're not just like all the other sales reps?

It's too early in the process to dazzle them with a presentation. You can't ensure relevance. Plus, "you" is not their favorite subject. So how do you quickly demonstrate you know more about solving the problem than the listener while wearing your journalist hat? The most subtle and effective way to demonstrate your expertise in the first few meetings, while remaining focused on the customer, is by learning to attach a disruptive truth to your question.

Here are a few examples:

"Three things drive employee engagement: autonomy, meaning, and mastery. How are you ensuring engagement, especially with your millennials, by communicating the why—the purpose behind this initiative?"

"Ninety percent of social media strategies fail because they invest in content and channels that don't reach the intended audience. How would you assess your current social media strategy?"

"Dramatic change happens one-to-one and not in a workshop. How are you planning to invest in developing your leadership team once the training initiative ends?"

"By working with the hundreds of medical professionals over the last five years, we've found that the most effective way to ensure HIPAA compliance is to automate ____ not ____. How is your staff currently managing patient information?"

The truth is disruptive if it is counterintuitive to conventional wisdom. Each one of these questions begins with a statement that demonstrates a unique insight on the problem but puts the focus back on the customer. Does the truth have to be disruptive? No. But as we learned in chapter 4, predictability determines impact. The more disruptive, the more you capture the attention of the audience and the more credibility points you score.

A disruptive truth followed by a thought-provoking question prompts the other party to think differently about the problem and, more importantly, think differently about you. For example: "This is no ordinary conversation with a product-pushing sales rep," thinks the customer. "There may be something for me to learn." The goal is to identify and catalog the best practices in the industry and the typical mistakes people make. Think less about what you sell and focus on what has to happen to solve the customer's problem. Most likely your solution addresses only a portion of the problem, but the decision maker isn't interested in solving part of the problem. If you have all the insights required to solve their problem, you become invaluable.

You have a unique advantage that your prospective customers don't have: you can talk to the competition. They can't. You also spend more time in the market than they do. In my experience, this is the most underutilized strategy readily available to every seller. If you seek to discover new information about your customer's business in every conversation, in six months you may know more about the market you serve than most CEOs.

Once you have developed your list of best practices and *disruptive truths*, ask yourself, "Would they pay for this information?" If so, link those truths to your library of questions. This is the most effective

way, early in the process, to shift from product peddler to thought
leader status.

L.E.A.D.

There is more to uncovering the truth than how we position our question. How we respond to what is shared is just as important. Now that
we explored how to "ask" well, we need to LEAD. LEAD is a helpful
acronym for responding in a way that motivates the speaker to share
more, to open up. Like creating a safe environment for a turtle to come
out of its shell, we need to create an environment where the customer
will tell you anything. You sell more when the customer is talking than
when you are talking.

> Listen: Change your agenda, clear your cache, and tune in to
> what's implied.
> Empathetically Acknowledge: To meet their greatest emotional
> need, validate the customer's point of view. Your goal is for
> the customer to say, "Exactly."
> Drop the Rope: Enhance receptivity by ensuring the customer
> is comfortable with sharing negative information (e.g., loyal
> to competitor, low interest).

If you effectively ask questions and then LEAD, the truth will be
revealed.

Listen

Everyone knows and believes we should listen to the customer. Like
a parent reminding a child to do their homework or chores, we've
"heard" it a hundred times. The issue isn't that we don't know to
listen; the problem is we forget to "clear our cache."

A few years ago, I had the opportunity to present our solution to the head of sales for a Fortune 500 company. I'll call her Susan. To determine our recommended solution and to gain a better understanding of the need, I flew to Miami to meet with a regional vice president. An hour into our discovery session with the RVP, I could see the need was great and our solution was a perfect fit.

As I was wrapping up the meeting, the regional vice president offered a bit of advice: "Susan doesn't like PowerPoint. She wants a training program that is very interactive. The other firm we are considering has a training program built solely on simulations. Susan liked that. So make sure you demonstrate that your program is very hands on."

Got it, I thought as I walked out the door. *She wants a lot of interaction and very little PowerPoint. Not a problem.*

I've been down this road before. I knew what the RVP meant. He says interactive; we pride ourselves on being interactive. The head honcho doesn't like PowerPoint. I get it. PowerPoint is needed, but it shouldn't be the focus of the training, just a guide to ensure everyone is on the same page. My close ratio is more than 90 percent. I haven't lost to the competition in years. I've got this. The truth, however, was that I had no idea what the RVP meant by "Susan doesn't like PowerPoint."

The data collected over the last twenty years of selling my solution led me to the wrong conclusion. My years of experience actually worked against me. Susan didn't want to limit the amount of Power-Point; she wanted zero PowerPoint. *None.* She *hated* PowerPoint. She didn't want a program that leaned heavily on interactive simulations. No, she wanted a program that was 100 percent interactive simulations. As soon as I turned on my computer and pulled up the introductory slide, the meeting was over. It was as if I began the meeting with a racial slur. Receptivity vanished. There was no recovery. Why? Because I didn't "clear my cache."

As you probably know, when searching online your computer stores up cache. It stores information for future use, which speeds up the downloading process, saving time. If your computer has already downloaded a picture of a hotel you recently visited online, no need to download again. The image is pulled from cache and appears instantly.

Our brain works the same way. We don't process information again that is already stored as cache. If we've heard ten customers share the same complaint about our company, we don't process the information every time as if it's hearing it for the first time. If they say they are interested in a feature of our solution, we instantly know the relevant "ad" to pop up in the conversation. Stored cache is pulled from memory, associations are quickly made, and you process what you are hearing more rapidly. Again, it saves time and energy. Expensive is associated with better quality. Cholesterol is associated with health problems. Jocks are ____. Computer people are ____. People from the South are ____. Based on your experience, your brain naturally filled in the blanks.

My brain was loaded with cache compiled from meeting hundreds of customers and prospects. As soon I heard familiar information, my brain filled in the missing pieces. "Sure, I know what you mean by interactive. Got it."

Slipping into familiar patterns of thinking is basically hearing what you expect or want to hear. It's the downside of experience. You hear the beginning of a customer story and your brain shuts off: "No need to download again." While this can improve efficiency as we navigate the world around us, our cache stored on our hard drive sabotages our ability to take the trip and truly listen.

The longer we're in our role, the more difficult it is to clear the cache. You have so much data downloaded over your life span. It's why many of the veteran reps we work with struggle to build receptivity. Their knowledge of their solution is impressive, but they struggle with taking the trip. If the audience is receptive and the message is on point, their experience offers an advantage. But if they fail to clear their cache, their brain says, "No need to download new information." Been there, done that, and the wrong ad pops up or we miss the meaning of what the customer was trying to communicate.

People with effective interpersonal skills know how to clear their cache. For them, every conversation is new, every person is unique. They resist the temptation to increase the processing speed: "Yeah, yeah, I've heard this objection before. You think we're too expensive . . . You think the cost to implement is too high. Here's why you're wrong . . ."

Instead, they stop, listen, and download the information all over again:

"Tell me what concerns you about the cost."

"Tell me about your current solution."

Yes, assumptions are dangerous, but there is another casualty of not clearing your cache. You send a message: you don't value the customer's point of view.

The opposite of listening is ignoring. Listening is a choice, not a skill. Most think listening is just about the exchange of information. It's not. It's a statement of what you value. You care enough to truly understand their unique message without hitting the fast-forward button, or you don't. That may not be your intention, but it is the message we send when consciously or subconsciously we don't resist the gravitational pull to self and tune out.

A line from the movie *Hector and the Search for Happiness* says it all: "Listening is loving." The health of my relationship with my wife, children, and fourteen grandchildren depends on my willingness to clear my cache. So is your relationship with your prospects and customers. You want to blow somebody's mind? Call them up, invite them to coffee, and listen to them. You will quickly rise to unicorn status.

Empathetically Acknowledge—If You Care, They Will Share

Think of a time when you were asked an interesting question, one that intrigued you—maybe about your job—from someone you just recently met. And while answering the question, the person seemed distracted. As if to say, "I know it's polite to ask a few questions but when are going to get back to my favorite subject?" Or after answering a question, the person's response had zero connection to what you just said.

"Yeah, okay, cool. You want to grab some lunch?"

They may have heard you, but you need to know they heard you. If not, the willingness to share declines. When the decision maker speaks, you may be captivated by what was said. You may thoroughly understand what was communicated. But if the decision maker doesn't know it, it didn't happen. And when it doesn't occur, communication shuts down.

Other-centered sellers know that their response to the customer's point of view, the customer's story, is the greatest opportunity to meet the person's greatest emotional need. By empathetically acknowledging the customer's point of view, receptivity begins to blossom. Communicating that you care can happen through body language, eye contact, or a genuine, verbal acknowledgment of the message sent. When selling over the phone or virtually, you have only one of these options, but that can be an advantage. You are forced to offer something more than a head nod and a smile. Regardless of your selling environment, if you want to discover the truth, others need to *feel* that you care enough to understand the message they are attempting to communicate and solve their problem.

So will acknowledging the speaker with a few "uh-huhs" and a couple of "gotchas" suffice? Nope. When the decision maker communicates a complex or important message, enhanced receptivity hinges on a more thoughtful response. We need to acknowledge not only what was said but what was implied. Here's a really simple example related to a personal relationship:

"How was your day?"

"Morning was great."

"Cool, glad you had a good morning."

In the example above, an acknowledgment was given, but it didn't indicate care. The listener just repeated back exactly what was communicated. It's better than an "uh-huh" or silence, but what does it lack? It missed acknowledging the deeper meaning. If you want to demonstrate that you really care, you pick up on what is implied.

"How was your day?"

"Morning was great."

"Sounds like you had a rough afternoon. What happened?"

This demonstrates to the communicator, "What you are saying is so important that I'm intently working to get the full meaning." Every other form of acknowledgment can be delivered without effort, but communicating what's implied sends the message that you value the speaker. Are you always correct? Of course not. Sometimes you miss the mark. If so, you get the added bonus of getting the correct information.

Let's say the decision maker says, "Things are tight right now and I'm really not sure if we can move forward for another six months." And you respond with, "Sounds like you will need to free up some funds or improve your profit margins before you can consider our solution?"

"No, I just meant I'm jammed. We are in the middle of ramping up our staff and everyone is focused on hiring."

"Oh, I see. Your top priority right now is focused on building and equipping your team. The timing will be better in July?"

"Exactly!"

By acknowledging what's implied, the interpreted message is confirmed or corrected. As we learned in the previous chapter, the goal is to hear the magic word *exactly*. By acknowledging, you confirm your assumptions are accurate. More importantly, the decision maker is no longer in the dark about whether you care. Your tone of voice is the primary channel for communicating empathy. This is why you can't fake it. To deliver a compassionate, caring response you need to feel what they are feeling—to reach a compassion state.

For example, let's say the decision maker shares, "We are in a complete rebuild mode. I don't think we will be able to invest in new technology for a few months." What you think next will reveal your motive and determine your ability to communicate empathy. If your only thought is, "Okay, I guess I need to make a note to follow up in forty-five days. Sounds like this may be a waste of time," the message sent and received will be, "I'm not interested in what's happening to you. I'm only interested in what I can sell you." Brutal, but true.

But if you care and tap into what the person is feeling, you can empathize: "I can't imagine building this business for the last twenty years and watching it dismantle. I wonder how his family is doing? I hope he's going to be okay. I remember when I went through something similar in the early 2000s. I wonder how I can help." You will demonstrate empathy. Empathy starts in the heart, not the head.

In one scenario, you acknowledge by saying, "Sounds like I should follow up in about a month and a half. I hope everything turns out okay. I look forward to reconnecting in November." Typical response. In another scenario, you empathetically acknowledge by saying, "Sean, I really do hate to hear what happened to your business. How difficult has it been? Is there anything I can personally do to help?" Of course, what you say is determined by the level of relationship, but that is secondary to the warmth in your voice.

Remember the focus here is the Unreceptive. Therefore, it's critical to place a higher priority on the person over the information we seek. If you do, you will discover buried treasure. By clearing your cache and listening, you are able to empathetically acknowledge the customer and soon information begins to flow. As you get closer to the truth, you may discover unpleasant information. This may be your greatest test. Can you resist the temptation to sell and drop the rope?

Drop the Rope

Recently, I attended a mini workshop being facilitated by an "expert." In the beginning, we were all participating, freely willing to answer the leader's questions. By the end of the meeting, it was crickets, and the reason was simple: Every time we answered the question, we were corrected. Sometimes we were even scolded for having the "wrong" answers. I quit playing, as did most of the other attendees.

This will happen for your customers too. If your customer gets punished with an unwanted argument, lecture, or scolding for sharing information that doesn't line up with your agenda, most won't share it next time. It's just not worth the effort. Therefore, instead of pulling them in the direction we want them to go, we drop the rope. If you "pull," they're not going to tell you:

"I really want something you don't offer."

"I don't like working with ____."

"I don't feel like you should charge for that."

"I'm probably never going to work with you. I've been talking to my brother-in-law's company."

Even if you are meeting with someone who loves confrontation and has no problem sharing bad news, you want to know *why* they feel this way. Regardless of their style, aggressive or passive, if they don't share their true point of view, you will never have the opportunity to address it.

In 1968, at the age of ten, Daryl Davis was pelted with bottles and rocks while innocently marching in a Boy Scout parade. At first he thought the attack was against the Scouts. But soon he realized, as the only black person in the parade, the bottles were aimed at him. He was bewildered and confused: "They've never met me, they don't know me, so why would anyone want to attack me because of the color of my skin?" No one ever explained why. He needed an answer to the questions "Why are they hitting me? What had I done wrong? How can you hate me if you don't know me?"

He sought answers in history books but couldn't get a satisfying answer to his question. As an adult, he realized—who better to solve this mystery than the leader of the Ku Klux Klan? In an incredibly bold move, he asked his secretary to set up a meeting with Roger Kelly.

Here's what Daryl Davis said about his strategy for the meeting: "I wasn't there to fight him. I was there to learn from him. Where does this ideology come from? Because once you learn where it comes from, you can then figure out how to address it." He said, "I'm not believing what they are preaching, but I am trying to learn and understand."

The meeting lasted for about an hour. Daryl didn't retaliate or defend. He just listened. Eventually Roger Kelly would join Daryl at his home for dinner. Even more surprising, Daryl began attending KKK rallies. In a CNN interview, Kelly said of Davis, "I will follow that man to hell and back. . . . Lot of times we may not agree with everything, but he respects me and sits down and listens to me. And I will sit down, respect him, and I will listen to him."

Notice the order. Even though every answer to Davis's questions on race was not only wrong but evil, Davis listened. "Respect is the key. Sitting down and talking, not necessarily agreeing, respecting each other (enough) to air their point of view. Because of my respect and willingness to listen. And because of this, he ended up leaving the Klan." That was Daryl Davis's first convert. Since then, he has converted more than two hundred KKK members. He's not a sociologist or psychologist but a professional musician who understands how to take the trip and drop the rope.

What I love about this story is Daryl's decision, like Martin Luther King Jr., to pursue influence over revenge. Many, like me, would read that story and think, "How could you respect and seek to understand a KKK leader? At a minimum, he needs a tongue lashing." Daryl clearly had a higher calling. Instead of using the meeting to unload his justifiable resentments, he chose to influence. And he's literally changing the world.

Wrong answers may feel like the relationship is moving in the wrong direction, but it's actually an opportunity. The sharing of negative information is a sign of trust. Think of it as a test: "I'll feed you a little sliver of truth and if all goes well, I'll tell you more." If no threat exists, more will be revealed.

Don't overcome, redirect, or challenge. Don't say, "Yeah but . . ." By uncovering the unfiltered truth, you are either building a foundation to be heard, or quickly disqualifying the prospects and saving yourself countless hours of wasted time. So, regardless of what they share, remember there are no wrong answers.

Customer: I really want something you don't offer.

Seller: Tell me a bit more about that. We may not have the best solution for you. My goal today is to just determine if we can help you ____.

Customer: I'm not really that crazy about the idea of working with your company. I've had a bad experience in the past.

Seller: I'm so sorry to hear that we dropped the ball. We've had some problems in the past. Tell me what happened.

Customer: It doesn't make sense why you would charge for that.

Seller: Candidly, it may not. For some companies I meet with, they don't see the value of investing in ____. My goal today is to determine what does make sense. Tell me about . . .

In each of these scenarios, the seller drops the rope. Using words like "may not," "determine if," and "could," or just simply not countering negative information, helps customers out of their "shell." To be clear, your response to the "wrong" answer is not to abandon the conversation, throw the towel in, or agree with the customer. The goal is to create a safe environment for truth to blossom. Again, think of your role as a journalist. Your agenda is not to overcome or change beliefs but to get the full story. Once you know the truth, and if the customer is qualified, later you will have the chance to switch roles and respond.

PART IV

THE FOURTH BARRIER—CHANGING THEIR BELIEFS

In discovery, our role is much like a journalist. But when attempting to change beliefs and build value in a recommendation, we become the evangelist, persuading the listener to see a better way. This section is about how to deliver a recommendation in the toughest environments to the most skeptical of audiences and how to navigate the barrier even the most seasoned sellers struggle to overcome: changing strongly held beliefs. Even if receptivity at this point is high, it can quickly evaporate if the recommendation is mishandled or fails to effectively identify and address the customer's concerns. It takes only a few words and poor decisions to derail the conversation or lose the deal.

TEN

Setting the Stage

*When presenting to an unreceptive audience,
your performance, not your solution, determines
if your recommendation is embraced. Therefore,
you need to set the stage.*

U p to this point, we have explored how to enhance receptivity to the message. Now, it's time to discuss how to deliver the message in a way that ensures you don't lose the audience and that will compel them to change their beliefs. It starts with setting the stage. Often, if you allow the customer to dictate the process, you will both lose. This was the case with a very competent seller for a marketing firm.

The rep was from one of two firms given forty-five minutes to make their online presentation. It sounds simple enough, right? The seller did what most sellers do. She said "yes, sir" and "yes, ma'am" and did what she was told throughout the process. She knew her stuff and competently presented the solution. What she didn't know was that she had lost before she even began.

It turned out the other firm was highly recommended by an existing vendor and, due to a warm referral, had already had multiple meetings with the ultimate decision maker. Her firm was found through a Google search and came in cold. Receptivity was obviously low. She lost when she agreed to this process and didn't ask for anything else. It was like she was asked to sing in front of five thousand people with no microphone while the competition had a full band and a killer sound system. Talent and skill didn't matter, and her preparation didn't help. She needed to control the stage or not play.

The second presenter knew exactly what to communicate about their solution. Given the rules of the game, as defined by the decision maker, the first presenter *never* had a chance. In a forty-five-minute presentation to complete strangers, it was impossible for anyone to unseat the firm that had the inside track. In other words, the rep may have had an amazing voice, but no one allowed her to "perform."

To change beliefs and win the deal, you need to first control the performance and set the stage. More specifically, you need to determine what information they need so you can cull what information you will share, how much time you require to demonstrate the value of your solution, and who should be there.

DETERMINE THE INFORMATION REQUIRED

All too often, sellers are asked to present to an audience they don't know, and because they have too little information about the problem or decision drivers, they often deliver a generic presentation. If you have a strong competitive advantage and you are meeting with a receptive decision maker, you may succeed. If not, this is not just a recipe for disaster but a complete waste of time. You need information to convert the Unreceptive.

Sure, early in the sales process it's reasonable to offer a generic presentation of "here's what we offer" to help the customer get a clearer picture of who you are. But if the goal of the presentation is to determine who wins the deal or if you want to change beliefs, unless you are the only game in town, blindly throwing darts at a board will fail a high percentage of the time.

To make the most effective presentation, you need to know three things:

1. What problem needs solving and how does the problem affect the business?
2. What criteria will be used to determine who will solve the problem (formal and informal decision drivers)? And who created those drivers (it's obviously helpful to know who is the decision maker or makers)?
3. What's best way to solve their problem (what's your recommendation)?

This was covered in chapter 8, but it bears repeating. If you can answer those three questions, you have a good shot at building the right presentation or building value in your solution. If not, don't perform. Sticking with our music competition metaphor, if you don't know the purpose of the performance, what kind of music they like, or if the person who chooses the talent isn't in the room, challenge the decision-making process. We'll come back to this later. To convert the disinterested, you not only need information but time.

DETERMINE THE TIME REQUIRED

Surprisingly, most decision makers don't have the experience to build the perfect process for vetting a solution. So if they lead, you are following someone who is lost. And way too often this results in a lose-lose scenario.

Based on the decision drivers, determine how much time is required to ensure the prospect can adequately assess the solution. If they need to see it to believe it, how much time is required for the decision-making team or decision maker to "see" it.

For example, if they need to meet the key members of your team or demo a product, determine how much time is required to do just that. Most sellers just take what they can get: "How much time can I have?" Instead, ask yourself, "What do they really need to see, experience, or understand in order to make the best decision?" Let that determine the time required. As Covey said in *The 7 Habits of Highly Effective People*, begin with the end in mind.

If the customer, like most, is unclear because they lack experience, then it's your responsibility to communicate and influence the customer to follow your recommended process, which may require adding steps to their decision-making process. If you are unsure of the right process or the time required, that's homework assignment number one.

DETERMINE WHO'S REQUIRED

As mentioned earlier, if the right people or person isn't in the room, what's the purpose of the presentation? To equip the attendees to sell your solution? Would you trust the outcome of an opportunity to someone you just met whose only knowledge of your solution is based on a ninety-minute presentation? Therefore, don't be afraid to ask the tough questions like:

- Who is driving and involved in the decision-making process?
- Who is the person who had the most influence over determining the decision drivers?
- What will happen after the presentation? Do you need to meet with anyone else?
- How will this project get funded? Will the person (i.e., the economic buyer) be in the room?
- Who could kill this deal?

Most sellers are tentative for good reason: they fear damaging the relationship with their main contact, most likely the evaluator. The person who *makes* it happen but not the person who *determines* what happens. I get it. It's a relationship that's critically important.

The key is to spend enough time with evaluators to ensure they shift from evaluating your solution to becoming an advocate. Simply put, sell them first. Once sold, you can begin working together on how to sell the solution to the rest of the decision makers.

If you are a late arrival to the party and don't have the opportunity to build an alliance, you are already in a very weak position. It's imperative you shake things up a bit and take some risk to win the deal. If not, you are most likely just practicing for the next opportunity.

POSITION THE WHY

The key to accomplishing all of the above boils down to answering the "why" question. Why is it in the customer's best interest to provide additional information, give you the time, add a step to the process, or allow access to the right people?

If you can't position your request as a way to help the customer make the best decision, it's seen as a manipulation tactic at worst or groveling at best. As we covered in the previous chapter, spend some time nailing down how to position your request:

"If you can provide more information about ___, I will be able to make a recommendation, not just a presentation. And I can focus my time on only what is most important to you."

"We have found that if the right people aren't in the room, we often struggle to ensure the solution will be backed by the executive team. Which, a high percentage of time, greatly diminishes ROI."

"For you to really assess our solution, or any solution designed to solve ___, you need to see how it works. We have found that the time required to ___ is about two hours. Again, my goal is to eliminate risk and for you to know exactly what you are buying—from us or the competition. There is way too much at stake to shortcut the process."

If you're passionate about helping versus selling, your enthusiasm and conviction will be compelling, and the right words will flow. The key is to check your motive—is it to help the customer make the best decision or just win a deal? Remember, your motive will ultimately be transparent.

DETERMINE WHEN TO SAY NO

I can hear you saying, "Yeah, Tom, in a perfect world I would know everything I need to know, I would get the time I need to demonstrate my solution, and I would have the right people in the room. But my world is far from perfect." Believe me, I get it. Especially when you are invited in late, it's common to be somewhat in the dark. If you have a competitive advantage and the odds are in your favor, it's wise not to fight the process. But sometimes you need to hit the brakes.

A few years ago, mine was one of ten companies invited to make a capabilities presentation to the learning team of one of the largest auto insurance companies in the US. I was promised that this was just an introductory meeting and more time for discovery would be allowed. According to my point person, the goal was to meet viable vendors and then narrow down the list to three or four qualified firms.

Given our experience in this industry and the role of the sellers, I was confident this would go well. I nailed my presentation and, based on the response, I was very confident I would move to the next round where I would learn more about the company and meet all the stakeholders. I was shocked when I got a call from the head of learning to tell me that I had come in second. They were going with the firm, the leader in our industry, they had chosen two years ago when the project got put on hold.

Obviously disappointed and feeling a bit manipulated, I did understand that sometimes this comes with the territory. But I was once again shocked a few days later when I got a call from the head of learning to explain a surprising turn of events. Instead of just accepting the learning team's recommendation, the CEO and COO had asked to meet with the two finalists. They requested I fly back the following week and make another presentation.

Of course I said I would love to, but I wanted to meet with several of the stakeholders and the COO before walking in cold.

I said, "My goal is to make a recommendation and not a generic presentation. For me to intelligently communicate how I can help your organization and not waste everyone's time, I need to know a bit more about . . ." I went on to explain why it was critical to set up a few discovery meetings.

She said no. I could tell by the tone of her voice that she and her team knew the other firm well and wanted to work with them. They'd basically already told me as much. This was just a mock exercise to appease the Cs.

I politely declined.

I knew it was impossible to ensure receptivity and deliver an effective presentation without first taking the trip. I'm not willing to burn hours of prep time, travel time, and cash to "sing with no microphone" when, the night before, the other firm had dinner with the decision makers.

Now, the point person had a problem. The CEO and COO asked for a meeting with the top two firms, and she had to make that happen. She eventually acquiesced and set up a few meetings for me.

By talking to the executives, not only did I learn more about their "whiteboard" and all the information described above, I also learned about their fascination with a leading marketing consultant at the time named G. Clotaire Rapaille. They had read his book and were big fans of his nontraditional marketing strategies. They were using his techniques to drive how the company marketed and sold their services.

So I read the book, then built my entire presentation around Rapaille's marketing principles and how our approach to selling aligned with their strategy. As I was walking onto the plane after the presentation, I got a call from the head of learning: we won the project. After the call, I got bumped up to first class. At that moment, all was right in the world.

Here's the truth about presentations: whether they're informal and to just one person or formal and to a group of execs in a boardroom, the best presentation wins, not the best solution. There's just not enough time to fully vet the solution. Therefore, there are situations in which you need to say no.

Be clear on what you need to deliver your truth. "I'm not 'singing' unless ____." Every time you are working on a deal, you are losing a deal. You cannot be in two places at once. It's up to you to determine if giving up your most valuable resource, time, is worth it.

Knowing when to say no is based on two questions:

1. If you don't have the information described above or aren't able to meet with the ultimate decision maker, will you lose?
2. Will the process defined by the decision-making team lead to a decision that will most likely result in a complete failure to solve their problem?

If you are going to lose anyway, or the decision-making process is so flawed that they will ultimately choose the wrong provider or a flawed solution, it's best to draw a hard line in the sand and say no.

"Fifty percent of the success of an initiative like this is based on ____. And without understanding more about ____ and having the opportunity to demonstrate ____, I'm just not sure how I can help you make the best decision. Are you open to changing your process?"

Here's the good news: in the few times I've created a fork in the road and boldly but graciously stated my requirements to participate, the customer changed their process, and I won 100 percent of those opportunities. Why did they change their mind? I think it primarily came down to understanding my motive. My goal wasn't to manipulate the process to win but to serve. I knew either I couldn't help them with the information available to me or the process was so flawed they were headed off a cliff, and it was my responsibility to make that clear.

Of course, like you, I always want to win. But the best way to accomplish that goal is to first focus on what's best for the customer. The simple truth is this: if you are the expert in solving the customer's problem, you should lead. If you aren't or act like you aren't, they will probably choose someone else and/or make a poor decision.

A Formula for Changing Beliefs:
Action = Belief + Care

Changing strongly held beliefs requires a radical departure from the traditional approach to building value. To prevail, reframe your role, your message, and your delivery.

For someone to dramatically change their beliefs, they not only need to believe change is in their best interest, they need to emotionally experience the benefit. This truth illustrates why very few save for retirement.

Do you believe in saving money for retirement? It's such an absurd question that I can't find a shred of research on the percentage of people who believe they shouldn't save money. It's akin to asking, "Who likes to take a vacation?" It's probably safe to assume that if you are breathing and over the age of thirty, you believe you should set aside money for the future. But here's the interesting thing: most people don't. Why do we say we believe in something and then not do it?

Fifty-three percent of Americans have less than $10,000 saved for retirement and 60 percent are spending all or more than they earn. And here's another interesting tidbit: 83 percent are shelling out a hundred dollars or more per month for TV and/or internet. So a large percentage of people who "can't" save money spend over a grand per year on cable. We all believe in saving, we all believe we should spend less than we make, but most don't. Why doesn't our behavior line up with our beliefs? Before I answer that question, think about something you believe you ought to do but you consistently fail to do. Unless you have tremendous discipline, there's an area in your life in which you truly believe change is needed but you regularly fail to act. Here's why.

To make a dramatic shift in our behavior, we not only have to believe change is needed, we also have to feel it. In other words, we have to care. Saving the necessary money for retirement and denying ourselves the temporal pleasures in life will not occur until we know what it *feels* like to be seventy and broke.

If you're twenty-two and know what it feels like to be seventy and broke, you'll max out your company 401(k) program. Maybe you're like me, and this doesn't dawn on you until you're fifty while watching your aging parents deal with financial stress. People are much less likely to embrace the pain of managing a budget when time is on their side. Instead, they're far more likely to believe ads that tell us life would be much richer and better if we owned the latest stuff and went to the hippest places.

Real behavioral change is determined not just by what we believe and know. For a dramatic shift in the way we act, we have to be emotionally connected to the reason for change. As the Heath brothers discovered in their research on what motivates people to *Switch*, their ground breaking book on the drivers to change, people don't think, analyze, and change. They see, feel, and change.

To influence people to make a dramatic shift in behavior, not just what toothpaste they buy but how they spend their hard-earned cash or why to give up something pleasurable, we have to appeal to both the emotional and the logical side of the brain. We need to know the ABC formula: Action = Belief + Care.

Let's start with beliefs. While emotions play a more prominent role in determining if your recommendation is embraced, we still need to address the logical side of the brain. To ensure the Unreceptive believe change is needed, we need to reframe our role, reframe our message, and reframe how we deliver our message.

REFRAME YOUR ROLE

In the hundreds of sales presentations I've observed, most people are very uncomfortable when first given the mic. There are lots of blank stares seemingly saying, "Dance monkey!" It's quite a different feeling than the friendly, casual dialogue about needs. I quickly realized early in my career that how I started usually determined where I ended. Good start, good finish.

Even if it's an informal one-on-one meeting in which you are delivering your recommendation, how you begin can determine the outcome. If you are uncomfortable, they are uncomfortable. Your emotional state becomes the focus and not your message. I found the simplest way to become grounded and demonstrate I am more focused on their needs than my performance was to boldly declare my role. This strategy was needed to win one of the most competitive opportunities I had ever pursued.

One of the largest communications companies in the country was looking for a company to transform their sales force. They started by assembling a team of more than ten stakeholders to assess the top fifteen potential sales training companies. Each was asked to submit an RFP (request for proposal). After the proposals were reviewed, the list was culled to five. We were one of the five. Next step, deliver a presentation to the decision-making committee.

This was a huge opportunity for our firm. A blue chip client and a large contract was on the line, but the odds were against us. We were competing against an incumbent, a firm who had a successful relationship with another division (the company was ten times our size). That firm's access to the decision-making team was high; our access was limited. We had a description of the need and desired solution but zero relational equity with the ten-person committee chosen to decide our fate. Receptivity was low.

This happens to all of us. What's the best strategy to change the odds? Start with your role.

What's your role? It's actually a very critical question. Is it to convince them to pick your company or just educate the customer on the solutions you offer? I think having an undefined or unspoken intent is where many of us miss the mark in creating receptivity. If we walk into a meeting or presentation without properly defining our role, gravity can easily pull us to a self-centered agenda, or the listener may assume we have a selfish motive. In both cases, receptivity is jeopardized.

This was my approach: "Believe it or not, our role today is not to convince you to choose ASLAN, although we would love that. Our role is to share what we've learned over the last eighteen years from other companies who have been down this road before. What we've learned about the best practices and mistakes to ensure you have the best plan in place to reach your destination. Hire us, don't hire us—of course, that's your call. Our focus today is to share with you what's required to transform your sales organization and double revenue in four years. Why is this our approach? Because we believe the best way for you to choose a partner is to understand what that partner knows about the problem you're trying to solve."

Before a presentation like this, I'm nervous and they're nervous. I'm nervous because I don't want to blow the deal or let my team members down. Customers are nervous because their name is attached to the decision to write a big check. If I fail, I lose a deal. If they fail, they may get fired.

The best way to alleviate that stress, for both parties, is to call a time-out and reexamine your role. For us, success that day became more about making sure they were completely prepared to tackle the challenge before them. I was entrusted with ninety minutes. If I never saw them again, my goal was to arm them with the best bridge to reach their destination.

It's radical. But once my role was clarified, I was no longer nervous. When my goal is not to earn a commission but to impart understanding, I am almost assured success, and therefore I'm no longer anxious. Sharing what I've learned is easy. Closing a deal is tough. Do I still want to win? Of course. But I've learned that my chances of winning increase when I choose to be other centered and change my focus from being chosen to serving my customer.

Let's check in on the client side. What happens as I switch roles from salesperson to unbiased consultant offering free expertise? Their receptivity to me and my message increases. If they believe I'm sincere, they no longer see me as a desperate sales rep but someone who is confident and passionate about what I do. I help people solve problems. They shift from hesitant adversary to eager note-taker. I become the trusted guide who is helping the hero of the story get what they want.

Will there be a time when I need to talk about my solution? Absolutely, but it is a smaller part of the story. The central theme is what people miss in their journey toward their desired destination. If I share what's missing, my solution to the problem will be assumed and the audience engagement is transformed. I end up responding to a request to know more versus shoveling a message into infertile soil.

Think about your presentation in light of what the customer will experience over several days of sales reps hawking their solutions. With this approach, you're almost ensured a competitive advantage. If your desire to serve is genuine, you will stand out.

After the initial presentation, we made it to round three and ultimately won a $1.5 million-dollar project. Did we win solely due to our informative and other-centered approach? Probably not. But when I asked the client why they chose our firm, the first thing they mentioned was the positive impact our approach had on the presentation. Our solution was important, but how we set the stage and organized the content around them, versus us, gave us the edge over firms who pitched "Here's who we are and here's what we do, and here's why you should buy our stuff."

They'd been around the block and already believed that there wasn't one company with a perfect prepackaged solution. They believed picking a solution provider who they could trust was as important as the solution itself. The client also understood that it was impossible to truly assess all the aspects of a solution in a ninety-minute presentation. They communicated that if they chose the right partner, the right solution would follow.

As stated earlier, the customer is buying you before they ever buy your solution. Remember, a key question that makes or breaks receptivity centers on whether the whole interaction is truly about them, or you. The very beginning of the presentation is the time to reveal your motive and answer that question definitively. You have a motive. If your audience doesn't know you, they will assume you are self-centered. Declare your other-centered intent.

Warning: if you are not genuine, the customer will know it and it will come off as a manipulation tactic, like a cheesy pickup line. If you mean it, they will sense your sincerity. Making the decision to change your role from winning at all costs to helping the customer determine what is needed to succeed changes you. You relax. Your facial expressions change. Your tone of voice changes. Your demeanor changes. You can't fake sincerity. People can tell when they are being worked. Your filter will eventually break down and your motive revealed.

REFRAME YOUR MESSAGE

It is possible for your prospect or customer to be truly captivated by every word you say? Yes, if you start with them. If you want to change someone's belief about retirement, don't begin with the benefits of saving a nest egg; start with their point of view.

Their Point of View

As you can see from Figure 5, this same framework we explored in chapter 4 about developing your Other-Centered Position is the same needed to deliver our message. We begin with their point of view, offer a disruptive truth, and then share our proprietary benefit. This is the most compelling way to make a key point, set up a slide, or tee up a product demo. And, as always, you start with the listener.

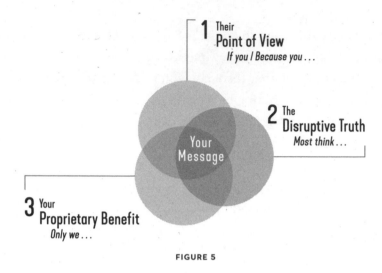

1 Their
Point of View
If you / Because you . . .

2 The
Disruptive Truth
Most think . . .

Your
Message

3 Your
Proprietary Benefit
Only we . . .

FIGURE 5

Once you've taken the trip with prospects, it's easy to jump from learning about their point of view to running back to your comfort zone, talking about your product. The instinct is to focus on why they need to change, a promise of a better life, better margins, more revenue, and so on. You see it so clearly because you now have the full story. The problem is, you may see it, but they don't. Their feet are still firmly planted on the South Pole, and if you instantly move to your other side of the planet, you will lose them.

Unreceptive people don't struggle. They are unwilling to burn brain cells to attempt to embrace something they don't believe. Like a missionary in a new country, you need to learn their language to have influence. To immediately capture their attention and ensure your prospect is willing to make the long journey to an unfamiliar perspective, start with what they care about, their point of view. As a reminder, here are three elements of the customer's point of view:

1. What they **want**—their desired destination

2. Their plan or **perspective** on getting what they want
3. Or a **problem** in getting what they want

Their perspective may include what they believe about you, the best path forward, or beliefs about the topic at hand. Resist the temptation to focus on what they *should* believe and instead focus on what they *do* believe. People you listen to, messages that resonate, or books that you love all articulate something you already believe. At the beginning of your presentation, draw them in by beginning the sentence "Because you . . ."

"Because you want . . ."

"Because you are challenged with . . ."

"Because you believe . . ."

"Because you've had a problem in the past with . . ."

If you can begin the sentence with those two words, *because you*, you will always get their undivided attention. Remember, if you show them a picture of themselves, they will look at it.

Of course, those two words aren't required, but when making a critical point, the need to start with their point of view is paramount. And if what you are about to say couldn't be prefaced with "because you," your message needs work.

I know there are times when you are speaking to a larger audience when discovery is limited or zero opportunity exists to discover their beliefs about you, your solution, or their current partners. Or maybe you have access but you know there's more to the story. Even if you're highly skilled at asking questions, you sense there are hidden fears, beliefs, and desires. That's great: other-centered communicators feel that tension. Those who feel that tension learn, seek, explore, and become surprisingly accurate at articulating the audience's point of view without ever shaking their hand.

If you question your accuracy or fail to get the assuring head nods, seek feedback and acknowledge their input. If it's a larger audience with limited audience participation, your humble attempt at communicating their viewpoint has much more impact than starting with what's most comfortable to you. As long as the overarching message is "I'm doing my best to focus on what is important to you," your mission is accomplished.

I've studied the great communicators over the last thirty years, and they all share a common trait: they can articulate the perspective of people they've never met. Exceptional communicators know what the audience is thinking about the topic at hand. They take the time to acknowledge the multiple perspectives audience members have. "It's as if she were talking to me," many of their listeners will say. How can they pull this off? They focus as much or more on learning their audience as they do on crafting their message.

When I first attempted to sell to Europeans, I struggled. I immediately became curious and wanted to understand why the same approach I used in America didn't resonate overseas. At every meal or social function, I asked questions about what they believed about Americans, what was unique about their culture, and the way they see the world.

The transformation was amazing. The scowls were replaced with smiles. As soon as I began to acknowledge my "Americanisms," the ice was broken. I became one of them. I was rewarded for doing my homework well. Because if I took the time to know, I must care. Because if I know and care, I will avoid the mistakes other Americans failed to avoid. Because if I know and am willing to change, I'm humble. Demonstrating that you know your audience says a lot about you. Again, they buy you before they ever buy your recommendation. And if you care enough to know them, you are someone to listen to.

The Farmer and the Shampoo Tycoon

The power of starting with the listener's point of view was nicely demonstrated by a billionaire on the TV program *Shark Tank*. In one episode, a hardworking man named Johnny was there to find a financial partner. He sauntered in to present to the sharks like he rode in on a horse. He was dressed in jeans, a T-shirt, a rodeo-style belt buckle, and a workingman's hat. You could tell he doesn't typically hang out with boardroom types.

He had been in the irrigation business for twenty-nine years, a business his father started, providing the equipment farmers need to water their crops. Johnny explained that water is not as plentiful as it was in the eighties, and farmers' costs are skyrocketing. His passion for farmers was obvious, but his resources were limited and the need was great.

Johnny was asking for $150,000 to expand his production of a product called the Tree T-Pee. It's a small dome that wraps around the base of the tree, reducing the gallons required to water a tree from 25,000 per year to just 850. He had a patent and had sold about 127,000 in a five-county area in Florida to his existing customer base. His margins are slim. He makes it for $2.95 and sells it for $4.50. He nets a buck on each Tree T-Pee.

Kevin O'Leary jumped in. "Why only $5? Why not charge $10 or $15?"

"Because I'm working with farmers. They're not buying one; they're buying five thousand," Johnny explains, as if to say, "I'm not doing that to my friends."

"Why not $7?" the shark continues.

"I've never done that. I've always tried to be right. If I sell seven thousand, I make $7,000." In other words, Johnny's primary goal is not to make more money. His point of view is to take care of the people he cares about.

O'Leary is interested but needs to convince Johnny to change his business approach, to change his perspective. Here's what the first shark communicated: "If I'm a big distributor of water irrigation systems and I see this product and you make it for $2.95 and sell it for $4.50, I can't get involved with you because there's not enough margin for me as a distributor. I need to be able to sell it for $12, at least. So

I can make some profit and you can make some profit. There's two mouths to feed."

"Yeah, but your selling to faaaarmers." Johnny draws out the word *farmers* as if to say, "Don't you get it? These people are not wealthy. They need our help." Why should I care about the rich distributor?

O'Leary takes another stab at getting Johnny to see his point of view. "I'm just exploring where your head's at. That means there's no room for a distributor who can pay more Johnnies to get out there and scale this out. Because you said all farmers need this, right? I need two thousand Johnnies all across the land. Who's going to pay them?"

You can sense the tension as Johnny digs in. Johnny is struggling to understand the shark's point of view. Because the first shark started with the distribution challenge (his point of view), Johnny resisted. All he heard was a business guy trying to make more money with no passion or real commitment to help the farmer. Johnny has a very unusual perspective. His goal is not to make more money but to find a way to help more farmers. Given that perspective, raising the price seems unconscionable. He believed there had to be a better plan than raising the price.

That's when a second shark, John Paul DeJoria, the founder of Paul Mitchell, chimes in. "Johnny, farmers are the cornerstone of America" (he starts with aligning with what Johnny cares about). "There may be a lot of farmers out there that can't afford $12 per tree [agrees with Johnny], but maybe [drops the rope] they could afford $6 or $7. I'm going to give you everything you're asking for. Your $150,000 for 20 percent. What you are doing is right [we want the same thing]. You deserve the chance to make it big and do a lot of good. I would like to be your partner, Johnny. I like everything you stand for. God bless America."

Johnny beams. He immediately agrees and walks over and embraces his new partner, a billionaire who understands and shares his passion for farmers. DeJoria understood the economics of getting distributors involved, but he focused on a completely different point of view,

Johnny's. Now that alignment has occurred, he has an opportunity to influence Johnny on the best strategy to get the product in the hands of every farmer in America. If the price needs to rise above $7, he has established a platform to have that conversation. The key was to start with Johnny's goal to help the farmer, not to help the distributor. Once alignment occurs, there will be an opportunity to reframe. If you can start a sentence with other people's perspective or problem, you will immediately get their undivided attention. Remember, the simplest way to think about it is—can you begin the sentence with "Because you . . ."? This is why DeJoria won Johnny over: "Johnny, [because you believe] farmers are the cornerstone of America . . .".

Robert F. Kennedy may have faced the most unreceptive audience in history. In 1968, he stood before a primarily black audience to make a statement on the heels of the assassination of Martin Luther King Jr. His goal was to demonstrate empathy, but he also wanted his audience to take action. He wanted them to return home, peacefully. As you can imagine, tensions were high. The country could easily erupt in riots. Here's where he began:

> Martin Luther King dedicated his life to love and to justice for his fellow human beings, and he died because of that effort. In this difficult day, in this difficult time for the United States, it is perhaps well to ask what kind of a nation we are and what direction we want to move in. For those of you who are black—considering the evidence there evidently is that there were white people who were responsible—you can be filled with bitterness, with hatred, and a desire for revenge. We can move in that direction as a country, in great polarization—black people amongst black, white people amongst white, filled with hatred toward one another. Or we can make an effort, as Martin Luther King did, to understand and to comprehend, and to replace that violence, that stain of bloodshed that has spread across our land, with an effort to understand with compassion and love. For

those of you who are black and are tempted to be filled with hatred and distrust at the injustice of such an act, against all white people, I can only say that I feel in my own heart the same kind of feeling. I had a member of my family killed, but he was killed by a white man.

Kennedy didn't try to avoid their point of view. In fact, he did just the opposite. He stated what they knew of Martin Luther King and how they must have felt. Instead of resisting what he had to say, they agreed. It was truth. How could they not feel "bitterness, hatred, and a desire for revenge"? That was their point of view. He felt the same. It had happened to him. His underlying message from the first few paragraphs of his speech was: we are together, not apart.

Also, notice how he drops the rope. The choice is clearly theirs: "You can move in that direction . . . or make an effort . . ." By not trying to control the crowd, leverage the law, or his position of authority, there was nothing to resist. He focused on what they wanted, not what he wanted. The decision is always theirs. What do they think they should do? The struggle isn't against the senator, a public official, or the law. It's with their conscience. What do *they* believe is the right thing to do? What would Martin Luther King do? He trusted them and they proved worthy of his trust. As most people do.

Whether the information is gained before meetings with the decision makers, interviewing similar customers, or from those who know your audience members, make it your goal to begin your presentation by blowing their minds with how well you know them. If you can get a few heads nodding, some knowing smirks (how did she know that?), and some "amen, sister, preach it," your likelihood of influence grows exponentially.

Not only do you need to articulate their point of view, it needs to move you. Like Robert Kennedy, you need to demonstrate that you not only understand what they think but how they feel. I've learned over twenty years of making presentations that if you make a sincere effort to start with and describe their point of view, even if you miss a few details, your stock with the audience still improves. They would rather help you struggle to understand them than be bored by details about you.

The villain in selling is the gravitational pull to your perspective, your agenda, and your desire to make a point. This is natural, but it inhibits your ability to influence. You spend countless hours thinking about the benefits of your solution. You go to your company meetings and they go to theirs. Don't ask them to struggle and learn your point of view; struggle to learn theirs.

This is why the majority of your prep time should be spent nailing down how you are going to articulate their point of view for every key point of your presentation. You have a huge library to pull from when explaining your solution. The next time you take the stage and there's that awkward silence, begin with their favorite "song." Even if you stumble a bit, they will offer grace as they see you struggling to make them the hero of the story.

Disruptive Truth

As we discussed in chapter 4, a disruptive truth can be a principle, best practice, or a bit of research that demonstrates an unexpected but better way to solve the customer's problem or get what the customer wants. Remember, our role is to lead customers to a better solution to their problem. By communicating new insights, you are someone worth following. Not only is there power in the words, you instill confidence when you communicate in definitive statements, such as:

> "If you want to move to transition to telemedicine, based on our study of more than 250 clinics, three things need to happen . . ."

> "By increasing customer loyalty by only 1 percent, you will increase profits by 13 percent."

"When companies implement a change initiative, the number one driver to success is how they communicate the 'why' behind change."

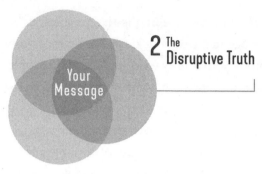

FIGURE 6

You are not selling, you are educating. Do you always have to share a disruptive truth? No, save them for the topics or points when receptivity to your recommendation is low (see Figure 6). If receptivity is high to the point you are making or the topic at hand, sharing the benefit of what you offer may be all that's required. Spend your time developing disruptive truths for the subjects where you typically see the most resistance.

In the first few years of sales training, due to my background, we focused exclusively on training inside sales organizations. One of our first large opportunities was a meeting with FedEx. It was 1997. Spice Girls were hot, but I was not. I worked out of my partner's basement with no windows. I didn't have a receptionist, employees, a real desk, or a brochure. But through my tenacious cold-calling efforts, I persuaded one of the training leaders, Mike, to let us provide a free mini workshop on objection handling. Halfway through the two-hour workshop, the head of inside sales at FedEx, a guy named Paul, walked in and sat in the back.

Through my earlier meetings with Mike, I knew FedEx had a training contract with a large, well-known training provider. And "corporate" drove all the training initiatives. Our chances of working with

FedEx seemed slim. The only benefit of the free training was probably a visit to Graceland.

At the end of the workshop, I had the opportunity to meet Paul. We chitchatted for a few minutes. I could tell he liked what he saw, but the subject of training was closed. As we were wrapping up the conversation, I said, "Paul, you are already working with a great firm, and the training provided by corporate is cost free to you. So I completely understand that working with another firm is probably out of the question."

He softened a bit. I continued, "As you know, selling exclusively over the phone is different. Because of that, we've been focused on developing training programs for inside sellers for the last five years. And we have learned that there are eighteen unique challenges of selling and managing customers via the phone. If you ever see gaps in what corporate is providing, I'd love to talk with you about what we've learned."

Paul did a 180. That statement opened the door to further discovery meetings and, ultimately, a large contract with our first Fortune 500 company. Notice the order of the first two elements of the most effective message. By starting with their point of view and a disruptive truth about how to solve their problem, you keep the story focused on the "hero."

"Because you . . . Most people think ___ but actually ____ is true."

This is why it's best to follow the process. Start with their point of view, followed by a disruptive truth. With this approach, you are perfectly setup to deliver a compelling, proprietary benefit.

Your Proprietary Benefit

As previously explored, proprietary benefit is defined as what differentiates you from the competition (see Figure 7). What are the unique benefits you offer that, if desired by the decision maker, give you the competitive advantage?

3 Your
Proprietary Benefit

FIGURE 7

Scores of books have been written on the importance of benefits (communicating a financial or emotional payoff to the customer). The focus here is what's different about you. Whether it's how you deliver the solution, your expertise, or a specific benefit of your solution, to convert the Unreceptive, you need to create contrast.

Yes, you will need to provide information on benefits offered by the competition. But if you spend your one- to two-hour presentation highlighting the same benefits offered by the competition, you may not only diminish receptivity, you will most likely lose to the low cost provider.

Over my twenty-five years of working with the top sellers in the world, I noticed one common denominator. They know the competition's as well as their own solution. Several years ago, I was working with the sales force of a large home builder. As part of our discovery process, I met with their top seller. I asked him the secret to his success. He paused and said, "I know my competition."

He went on to explain that a large, competing home builder had just moved into the market. He said there was a lot of chatter among the sales reps about what this would mean to business, how this could hurt their business. He said, "I toured their homes. I want to know everything they offer, down to the wallpaper, so I can help our customers determine how we are unique."

Notice the order. Even when you are building value, customers are first; your solution comes last. It's other centered. You start by describing what is important to *them*, you then share a helpful, unknown truth about a better way to solve *their* problem, and then last, you communicate how you can uniquely solve *their* problem or help them get what they want. And by starting with their point of view, it guarantees that your benefit is actually a benefit. There is no better way to deliver a message to a skeptical listener. Now, let's bring all these ideas together in a relevant example.

Let's say the solution offered by the seller is a coaching automation tool that simplifies and improves how frontline managers measure performance and develop their team (think CRM for managers). The customer's problem: due to the challenge of selling a very competitive service, the sales force is struggling to hit their quota and turnover is high.

The VP of sales (the decision maker) point of view: it's a rep problem. The learning team is recommending a training solution. He is primarily looking for a rep solution for a rep problem. Beyond a training program, he is also looking into improving their hiring process. Here's how a seller leveraged this framework to kick off the initial meeting and ultimately win a million-dollar-plus contract.

Point of View: "Your turnover is skyrocketing, the highest level in history—more than 30 percent. And revenue is suffering. The belief of the learning team is that it's a rep execution problem. Therefore, you need to provide training for your sellers."

The VP leans in: "Exactly."

Disruptive Truth: "Here's what we've learned when working with similar organizations. Dramatic change happens one-to-one and, unfortunately, not in a two-day training workshop. Training is needed to ignite the desire for change and skill development, but leaders ultimately determine rep engagement and lasting behavior change. One hundred percent of the organizations that have been successful in transforming their sales force prioritize leadership development and providing the tools they need to coach, above rep development. It's less expensive and it's more effective."

VP: "Tell me more."

Proprietary Benefit: "Today, if you are open, I want to share our Catalyst solution. It was developed to equip frontline managers to address the four barriers of engagement, accurately measure performance, and provide a simple recipe to bridge the gap in rep performance. It has more than one hundred developmental activities specifically designed for hunters [their term for describing the rep's role]. You will see that it reduces the cost of training by investing in the people who are more committed to the organization, and it is the quickest way to reduce rep attrition."

Obviously much more was communicated and discussed, but you get the picture. The seller started by articulating the decision maker's point of view. The disruptive truth helped the decision maker see a better, more cost-effective way to solve the problem. Additionally, the solution offered clearly communicated a unique approach: What are the four barriers to change? The seller knew that no other company could offer the more than one hundred developmental activities specifically designed for sales reps.

Again, notice the order. Given the need to alter how the VP thought about the best solution, just diving into the Catalyst solution would have been met with immediate pushback.

The VP's need to improve the hiring process may be a problem, and the seller did offer a solution to address it, but it wasn't proprietary. He knew that the best solution for the VP was the Catalyst solution, and in time, they would explore additional services offered by their company.

As you work on this, don't get discouraged. This is an advanced skill. To convert the most difficult audience, whether a teenager at home or the toughest customer, the traditional approach of communicating only features and benefits will fail. Start by developing a table that begins with a list of your solution and proprietary benefits. In the next column, define the relevant problem. In the last column, develop your list of disruptive truths.

With your list developed, choose just one to practice in your next meeting, or better yet, practice with a friend or a coach. As you get more comfortable, add another. It's better to be present and natural with the customer than thinking through a new model.

Lastly, remember all three elements are not required. At times, you can be successful in just creating contrast and communicating a proprietary benefit. But when receptivity is low, remember to follow the process, always tying everything you communicate back to their point of view.

REFRAME YOUR DELIVERY

How you deliver your message is just as important as the message itself. A poorly delivered message, like food delivered in a dirty box, will most likely be repugnant to the listener. If the message is delivered poorly, it is most likely because of the position we assume when making our recommendation. Sellers who struggle with effective delivery either take a superior position and speak down to the customer or position themselves as inferior. Our goal is to approach the person as a peer, regardless of rank or power.

I often attend networking conferences. It's a form of speed dating for business executives who desire to meet numerous suppliers in one location. The event planner matches vendors with companies potentially needing their services. For two days, you bounce from one thirty-minute meeting to the next in hopes of quickly engaging a handful of very qualified prospects.

At one event, all the vendors gathered to hear instructions from the director of the conference. When the topic shifted to "How to sell your services," I started to tune out. Been there, done that. I don't need any help about how to sell a company I started twenty years ago, I arrogantly thought. My receptivity was low, and if the event planner had started off with a "teacher-speaking-to-students" attitude, she would have definitely lost me. But she didn't.

"I know you all have a lot of experience and certainly don't need advice on how to sell your services. But I wanted to share something we consistently hear from the delegates [my prospective prospects] who attend these conferences. They often tell us that they are put off by being contacted by your sales rep. They consistently request that the next step be with the person they initially met with. Once a warm handoff is made to your sales team, they are fine with continuing the relationship with the account manager. Again, I know this is something you would most likely never do, but it's always good to be reminded."

In fact, I had made that mistake in the past. I did need to hear that message. And because of the way she communicated the information, as a peer, I was incredibly receptive to the message. Think of the alternative way this message could have been communicated. "First, let's cover several mistakes I often see vendors make when trying to sell your services. To effectively evaluate this conference, it will come down to the number of deals you close. So here are the three keys to selling your service . . ."

Sadly, if this had been the approach, I would have resisted the needed advice, thinking, "I don't need Sales 101 advice. I teach selling skills for a living."

Instead, she was just passing on information she'd heard from her previous clients. She knew people don't respond well to unsolicited advice, so she couched it as shared insight and respectfully acknowledged our experience.

If, like me, you tend to lean to the superior position, driven by the need to impress your clients with experience and demonstrate you have the expertise to solve their problem, when offering advice, think of starting sentences with the words *I*, *we*, or *they* versus *you*.

When the sentence starts with *I*, it rarely causes dissension, and my message is typically embraced. Starting with *I* tells my wife that what follows is about me and not a complaint about her. When talking to a customer, it has the same effect.

"Over the years I've learned that the most successful companies we've worked with never skip this step. If they do, it historically leads to an increase in . . ."

"I was recently talking with a client, and they shared that when they implemented . . ."

"In my previous role as a ____, I overlooked a key step in the process, and it resulted in losing a month of productivity. Your organization may be different, but I wanted you to be aware of . . ."

Avoid "You need to . . ." or "You should . . ." or "You will make a mistake if . . ." When attempting to persuade someone to change beliefs, you are essentially pointing out that they are wrong. Most people don't like being told they are wrong. To change this perception, you have two options: (1) share where you have failed and/or (2) share what others taught you.

When advising my children in their teen years or even sometimes now as adults, I focus on how I failed at the topic at hand and what I learned from my experience. Or I reveal what my father, mother, or friend taught me. This establishes equality and removes the perception that I am superior.

The key is to tune into how your words and tone establish your position in the conversation. Are you above them or are you beside them? Do you appear humble or arrogant? For most, negative emotions surface if your delivery triggers memories of conversations with parents, teachers, preachers, coaches, and bosses. Any approach that places you above the listener is dangerous.

Another way to think about this is to share the news, not your opinion. It's also helpful to drop the rope when delivering your recommendation or advice.

"This may be helpful; one of my clients shared this with me."

"Investing in ____ is what provides the highest return on investment for most of my clients. But, of course, I am happy to discuss other options that may be a better fit for your organization."

"Do you mind if I share something with you that we learned from a research project we conducted about similar companies in your industry?"

To be clear, dropping the rope is not recommended when talking about who you are, the value of what you offer, or what you've accomplished. No one is asking you to water down the truth here. Those important points need to be stated passionately and confidently. But you will most likely lose the customer if you pull the rope by telling the customer what to do. You are offering a recommendation, not making a command.

If you lean toward a more passive approach (that is, being a manager versus a rep), when you can tend to take an inferior position, learning how to share your recommendation will give you the comfort to speak up. Your concern for stepping on the customer's toes and trying to avoid conflict or uncomfortable conversations is valid. If you share the news and drop the rope, you can deliver your message in a beautifully wrapped package. This should help address your concern of offending the customer while more naturally putting you in the position to lead the customer to the best solution.

Another tip for ensuring the message you want to deliver is actually the message received is to shift your focus from what you say to what is heard.

Focus on What They Hear, Not What You Say

I once observed a presenter turn off a significant portion of the audience simply by leaving out two words. The speaker's impressive track record in the industry was enough to convince anyone in the audience that the information being shared would positively affect their business. Everyone was engaged and receptive to the message until two words were excluded in a simple, off-the-cuff example. Those two words were: *Girl Scouts*.

The speaker made a simple reference to Boy Scouts without mentioning the other equally important Scout group. At once, many of the women in the room shut down. Despite his years of experience, a portion of the audience's receptivity vanished.

By not mentioning the Girl Scouts, some audience members viewed him as sexist. The assumption wasn't that he forgot to mention the other group because he had three sons or that it was just a simple mistake while standing in front of 150 people. He wasn't given that benefit of the doubt. No, unfortunately the message he accidentally delivered sabotaged his intended message. The costly mistake was due to filter malfunction. When on a platform, whether small or large, filter your message for how it could be interpreted. Receptivity can easily be lost right before the sale if we fail to focus on what people hear.

My wife often forgets to lock the back door and turn on the alarm. As I walk in the bedroom to remind her, I pause. How will she hear the message I'm about to deliver? "Hey, you need to lock the back door. And by the way, the alarm wasn't turned on." Because I know her, she will hear, "You're incompetent. Can't you even remember to lock the door?"

So I pause, revise, and go with, "I know you don't get scared at night, but it worries me to think about being out of town and you're home alone with the alarm off and the door unlocked. Will you do that for me?"

With this approach, two important messages are delivered and received: "You are loved and remember to lock the back door . . . for me." Not only does she agree, she feels more loved. It only took me about fifteen years of marriage to learn this, but at least I'm getting better. Does it take a little extra effort? Yep. But it's worth it. The tongue can be one of the most dangerous weapons on the planet, and without tuning our filter to what other people hear, it can cause devastation and undermine our ability to influence.

If you say, "I can't" to a customer, they hear "won't."

If you say, "I can't tell you the price," they hear an attempt at deception.

If you say, "This offer ends today," they hear a person focused more on commission than helping the customer make the best decision.

If you say the word "again," they hear, "You are not listening," or, "You aren't smart enough to get it the first time."

If you laugh when clients don't understand what you are trying to communicate, they may hear, "You're an idiot."

Think about a sales situation where decision makers talk positively about their current vendor. What will they hear if you bash the competition? If the decision was theirs, it's tantamount to asking a person who just showed up to a party, "Why are you wearing that?"

If face-to-face, your posture and body language send a message as well. I once had a VP ask me, "What's up with your arms being folded?" His tone wasn't curious. He was clearly annoyed. I apologized and explained that I had neck problems and folding my arms helps support my neck. He didn't hear from my body language "bad neck," he heard, "Tom's not really enjoying this conversation." I haven't folded my arms since.

Like me, we all struggle to be aware of how we deliver our message, in tone, words, or posture. It's helpful to listen and watch yourself. Record your next Zoom meeting or record the meeting on your phone. If you are like me, watching our hearing yourself isn't a very enjoyable activity, but it's what the top performers do in any industry.

No one's filter is perfect, but if listeners sense you are continuously striving to be fair and respectful in your message, they may overlook a few mistakes. By choosing to be an other-centered student, the filter gets incredibly accurate at anticipating how the audience will interpret the words you are about to deliver. The more you care about them, the more you take the trip, the more you will instinctively understand how they will interpret certain references or words. Your relationships will be richer, and the barriers are removed from accomplishing your ultimate goal, delivering the truth.

TWELVE

Word Pictures and Success Stories: Making the Emotional Connection

Once someone believes change is needed, to act on that belief, they must emotionally experience the benefit.

If you demonstrate that you understand customers' problems and offer a unique solution but fail to elicit emotion, they may agree but fail to act. "You're right, I should save for retirement . . ." "I should drink more water . . ." "I should invest in . . ." But secretly you both know, they probably won't. They believe it, but they just don't care enough to endure the pain required to change. The feeling may originate from the payoff of what they may get or from the fear of what they may lose, but the feeling is the driver behind acting on your recommendation.

The most effective and efficient way to get someone to emotionally experience the benefit is to make a connection with something the listener *cares* about and connect it to your recommendation or the point you want them to embrace. I call this association word pictures. They are pictures painted with words that ensure the listener can see something they were previously blind to. It's a powerful blend of an analogy and story that, if done correctly, elicits a powerful emotional response.

WORD PICTURES

My favorite example of a word picture was developed by a seller to persuade the customer to change their opinion about working with someone outside the industry. The customer's perspective: "I need to work with someone who understands our industry. There's just too much to learn. How can they help us if they don't understand the intricacies of health care?" It's a very valid point of view. Here's how the senior seller responded.

"Do you remember when the Houston Astros were on the cover of *Sports Illustrated* in 2017, predicted to win the World Series in 2017, and then they actually won in 2017?"

The decision maker grinned as he thought about how the Astros won. He was not only an avid fan but a former baseball coach.

The seller continued, "How did that happen? Why did *SI* predict this outcome?"

The customer responded enthusiastically, "Partially because they hired Sig Mejdal in 2012 to become Director of Decision Sciences. He completely changed the strategy for how they recruited players and built their roster."

The rep grinned. "Exactly, and because he wasn't an insider, and knew very little about baseball, he was able to see the problem through a completely new lens and came up with the best way to solve the Astros problem—build a winning team with minimal resources."

There are so many positive things happening in this example. First, think about how this shift from the business topic at hand activates the reticular activating system (RAS, in chapter 4). The customer likes where they are going but isn't sure where this is leading. It's a mystery, and the brain needs to solve a mystery.

More importantly, she drew on the emotional connection to the Astros winning to hiring an outsider. The seller leveraged something the customer understood and associated it with what the customer didn't understand or believe—why to hire an outsider. It instantly changed the beliefs of the customer. Another benefit of word pictures is how efficiently the point was made. This was not only effective but enjoyable for both. In forty-six words, emotions stirred and a strongly held belief was changed.

At fifteen, my daughter Tindell made a series of bad decisions that shifted from the typical teen rebellion to dangerous behavior. She was hiding alcohol in her room, smoking pot, and her attitude around the house was almost unbearable. We felt we were losing her and were willing to try anything. A friend suggested we take her to JH Ranch in Northern California. It was a daddy-daughter retreat where the day was filled with fun adventures, horseback riding, river trips, hiking; I even threw in a side shopping trip. At night, gifted speakers delivered messages designed for teens about living a better life. Tindell was interested in the days, and I was most interested in the nights. To my shock, she agreed to go.

About midweek, we went rafting down a river with some fairly dangerous rapids. At one point, the guides stopped all the rafts, and we waited for fifteen minutes while a few of them went ahead of us. They set up ropes and positioned themselves to ensure no raft could get caught in a particularly dangerous spot. As we were waiting, our guide explained that several people die every year because the current in this particular section of the river can trap the inexperienced rafter in seemingly tame water. You couldn't see it, but about three feet below the surface, the current was dangerously powerful as it was forced to flow between two large, submerged rocks. If you got near it, it would suck you under, lodge you between the two rocks, and you would drown. As we passed by, we were all shocked to see how, on the surface, there was no appearance of danger. This little adventure sparked an idea.

One of the last planned activities was a private hiking trip with your daughter. Once we reached a good place to sit and soak in the view, I asked Tindell if I could share something. I wanted her fifteen-year-old mind to comprehend the dangers of some of the decisions she was making. I wanted her to know I was no different or better than her. I wanted her to trust me. The river trip provided the perfect word picture.

"Tindy," I said, "I know this an obvious question, but hang with me. How did the guides know where that dangerous rapid was and how to avoid getting trapped between those two rocks?"

She responded, "They're experienced guides. They've been down the river before."

"Right," I said. "As we end the trip, here's what I want you to know. I know it may be hard to listen to your father, but I've been down the river before and I know where all the rapids are. I'm probably not any smarter than you and certainly not any better than you. My whole goal is to keep you from getting hurt. I just want to tell you where the rapids are. I've gotten caught in a few and seen others sucked under. My only goal is to share with you what I've seen. You can use the information to avoid the rapids or you can decide to figure it out for yourself. I just want to save you from some of the pain your mom and I have experienced in the rapids of life."

This led to a very open conversation and productive talk about sex, alcohol, drugs, and relationships with friends. It had such an impression on her, she wrote about it in her book and still refers to it in her thirties. It was powerful, because she had emotionally experienced the danger of the unseen rapids. It wasn't a logical conversation about the dangers of drinking; it was an emotional conversation about life and death. This is when I really learned about the power of a word picture.

Was there an immediate transformation after my little talk? Of course not, but the message stuck with her. The transformation occurred slowly over the next few years. But because of what I learned about all the truths shared in this book, regardless of her behavior, the relationship stayed strong, and she was always receptive to my perspective. A well-crafted word picture can be an incredibly effective tool for eliciting emotions, but there's another benefit of word pictures. They can also explain a complex topic in a just a few short sentences.

SIMPLIFY THE COMPLEX

I've been looking to replace the Rolex my father gave me when I graduated college ever since it tragically came off my wrist when I was pushed into a lake in 1988. I loved that watch. It always reminded me of the man I most admire. But with four kids and now fourteen grandchildren, it's hard for me to justify spending that kind of money on something I really don't need. But I still like to look.

This explains why I wandered into a store filled with expensive shiny things a few months ago. While looking at a watch that I was sure would make me as appealing as the celebrity spokesperson, I asked the sales guy a question that has always puzzled me about watches: "What's the deal with Swiss movement? Why does the 'movement' matter?" His response was, "It's like engines. You take a 350 . . ."

I tuned out. I had no clue what he was talking about. I don't know anything about engines. What was already confusing got even more complicated. Now there are two topics I'm confused about, engines and Swiss movement. The seller's idea to use an analogy was good, but his execution was poor. We all have the challenge of explaining a complex concept in very little time. To simplify the complex, use word pictures to help customers picture or see something they don't understand.

Recently I was talking to a participant in one of my workshops when he pulled out an e-cigarette. To strike up a conversation, I said, "So what's up with vaping? Is it the same as smoking a cig?" As if I just smoked a pack of cigarettes with a few European hipster friends wearing skinny jeans.

He explained it to me instantly and brilliantly. "You ever tried turkey bacon?"

"Yeah, sure."

"Not as good, right?"

"Yeah, it's kind of like bacon, but I would much rather have the real thing."

He just nodded.

Notice the two components included in this simple word picture. The story was about me. Don't miss that. Your customers are always interested in a story where they are the central character. Also, the word picture leveraged something I understood, turkey bacon, to explain something that I didn't understand, vaping. As with a few of the word pictures shared previously, the first component is something to reach for but is ultimately optional. The second isn't. As always, if you are other centered, the effective word picture will naturally develop. The watch salesman was the center of the engine story. Because *he* likes engines, it's his go-to story. What if the watch salesman had made me the center of the story?

"You like engines?"

"Is that the thing under the hood?"

The watch seller tries again. "What about Champagne?"

"Not really," I respond but am still intrigued. Since I'm the focus of this word picture scavenger hunt, I'm leaning in.

One more try: "What about bourbon?"

Bingo! I do love a good bourbon.

Now that the seller, in this fictitious scenario, has dialed in on the right analogy, he could leverage what I know about how Kentucky controls and manages its high standard for crafting a great bourbon. He could explain as I connect pleasant memories of drinking bourbon with my friends, "As you know, whiskey can't be called bourbon if it isn't made in Kentucky following their standards for crafting a great whiskey. The same is true for any watch described with Swiss movement. Only watches made in Switzerland, complying with their high standard for building the best watches, can advertise Swiss movement."

I would have smiled, thinking, "Cool. I didn't know that. Makes perfect sense. Thanks, watch guy!" Leveraging something I already understand to explain something I don't requires little to no effort for the listener. E-cigs were explained to me in five words: "You ever tried turkey bacon?" As Herbert Simon, the Nobel Prize–winning economist, pointed out: when there's a wealth of information, there's a scarcity of attention. We are all overwhelmed. Our brain wants to burn as few calories as possible processing information. To ensure our message is heard and understood, we must fit within the customer's frame of reference or we will lose the receptivity of the listener.

Word pictures are like jokes. If further explanation is required, you missed the mark. Be careful using real scenarios, companies, movies, TV shows, or products as word pictures. If the audience knows all the facts, it undermines your point if the connection you're trying to make requires some finagling. "Well, I know the Astros didn't have a great year in 2017, but they won more games in 2017 than 2014. Yes, they came in last place but . . ." Because they did win the World Series in 2017, the word picture worked beautifully.

Are word pictures always required? No, at times they are just a tool to efficiently deliver your message. Here's a good rule of thumb. Invest the time to develop word pictures when:

1. Receptivity to your recommendation is low;
2. Communicating a complex idea that is difficult to grasp; and
3. It is imperative the customer understand ambiguous data or facts.

When receptivity is low and the distance the listener needs to travel to see an alternative point of view is great (as in case of my daughter), the word picture must stir emotions: "The rapids were scary. People died!" The longer they must travel to see your viewpoint, the more they have to care about reaching the ultimate destination. If clarity is your main objective, evoking emotions is not always required. All you may need is a simple word picture to keep the brain from burning as few calories as possible or to allow more time for other important topics.

Imagine the following:

You work for a company that sells voice and data services. You're calling a firm that uses a lot of data. Your goal is to convince them to increase their monthly cost by 15 percent to increase their download speed from 5MB to 10MB. Those facts alone mean nothing to most people. You need a word picture to illustrate what it will feel like to double their speed.

Your service is 20 percent more expensive than the main competition. You need a word picture to illustrate the added value they will receive for their extra investment.

You have very limited time to explain a complicated change in service—like a complicated pricing model. You need a word picture.

You're talking to your teenagers about the dangers of sex and the statistics related to STDs. You need a word picture.

Despite limiting his territory to a sixty-mile radius in his hometown of East Liverpool, Ohio, Ben Feldman was the number one life insurance salesman of his generation. In fact, in the '70s and '80s, he sold more life insurance than 1,500 of the 1,800 agencies in the country. Why was he so successful? He was tenacious and had an incredible work ethic, but so do others. Psychologist and bestselling author Robert Cialdini was so fascinated by Feldman's extraordinary success that he wanted to know more. Here's what he discovered and wrote in his book *Pre-Suasion*:

According to chroniclers of that success, he never pressured reluctant prospects into a sale. Instead, he employed a light (and enlightened) touch that led them smoothly toward a purchase. Mr. Feldman was a master of metaphor. In his portrayal of life's end, for instance, people didn't die, they "walked out" of life—a characterization that benefitted from associations to a breach in one's family responsibilities that would need to be filled. He was then quick to depict life insurance as the (metaphorically aligned) solution: "When you walk out," he would say, "your insurance money walks in." When exposed to this metaphoric lesson in the moral responsibility of buying life insurance, many a customer straightened up and walked right.

The guy who sold $15 million in life insurance in twenty-eight days while he was hospitalized for the month of February with cerebral hemorrhaging dropped the rope and used word pictures.

Creating Word Pictures

To build your library of word pictures and better explain this to your customers, here are a few ideas to get started:

- Figure out and rank the most difficult but important concepts required to sell your product, service, or solution.
- Set aside time to develop three to five word pictures for your most critical but complex concepts. Why so many? Some people hate sports analogies but love cars. Some hate cars and sports but love cooking or wine or music or politics. Try to develop a few word pictures that will appeal to every type of customer.
- Lastly, test it. Some of the seemingly best word pictures fall flat when delivered live. Like all good comedians, find a few friends to test out your material and refine your analogies accordingly.

SUCCESS STORIES

A more common approach to moving the customer to care is using stories of past success. They require less creative energy and can be just as effective. In his book *Building a Story Brand*, Donald Miller offers an effective template for creating a success story based on the scripts of the most popular Hollywood movies. If you follow the formula, it may be predictable and snubbed by the critics, but it works. Here's my simplification of the Hollywood formula for creating an effective story.

Scene one—The desired destination: The hero of the story wants something but is unsure of how to turn the vision into reality. Think of customers standing on a cliff, wanting to get to the other side, with the canyon below. How will they reach their desired destination? The listener gets emotionally connected to what's at stake, puts themselves in the story, and cares about what the hero wants.

Scene two—Meeting the trusted guide: They meet a guide who will help them get what they want. The wise person, the confidant who is trusted, who cares about our hero, and knows the way. You are the guide.

Scene three—Facing the villain: This is where they face the dragons, the challenges that arise as the hero makes the journey to the desired destination. Every great story has a villain. The listener becomes aware of the consequences of failing and the rewards that await if their vision becomes a reality.

Scene four—Happy ending: The hero wins the day, saves the planet, defeats the bad guy . . . or saves $20,000 in taxes.

As you build your story, remember, the brain loves to solve a mystery. Cialdini explains that mysteries "grab the reader (or the listener) by the collar and pulls them into the material. When presented properly, mysteries are so compelling the reader can't remain an aloof outside observer." The RAS demands that the mystery be solved. The brain wants to close the gap to make sense of the world. It's why we have to see what happens in the next episode or we hang on through the commercial break. "After the break, you will hear how one major Hollywood star attacked the crew that shut down production of their latest movie." The brain yearns for closure. "What Hollywood star? What did they do?"

One of the most successful ad campaigns of all time was a simple billboard that stated, "I Found It," which included a phone number. Millions of people had to know, "Found what?" The ad was run by a Christian organization, Campus Crusade for Christ. Tens of millions called and 3.5 million people converted to Christianity. Whether you support the cause or the strategy, it worked.

When crafting your story, use vivid imagery to activate the emotional side of the brain. Facts alone aren't compelling. People see, feel, and then act. Your objective is to create a mental picture. You want the customer to see the story, not slog through a financial report. You don't watch your favorite movies over and over again because of the information delivered. You watch because of how they make you feel. This is the hallmark of a great story—it should illicit emotions.

Consider how you would tell the story of a company that paid 20 percent more for a solution than the nearest competitor, but realized a 400 percent increase in profit margin. Those are great numbers, but numbers alone don't evoke emotion. Here's an example of how you could bring those numbers to life in a story about a small business owner named Melanie.

Scene One: Melanie is the owner and chef of Sonoma, a successful restaurant in Raleigh, NC. She wanted to expand. Her business was doing well, but she had a passion for becoming a successful entrepreneur. She wanted out of the kitchen and to build a restaurant group of ten restaurants. Cash was tight and she was working long hours. She missed her family.

Scene Two: Sonoma was referred to us because of our experience, our track record in moving businesses like hers from little to no process to automating all functions of the restaurant so they could replicate and grow, consistently repeating the secret sauce that lived only in Melanie's head.

Scene Three: We assessed all the functions of the restaurant, and there were major gaps, from how alcohol was managed to payroll: everything was a lot of tribal knowledge with no defined processes. If they wanted to grow, they could not repeat their success. If they expanded, their slim profit margin could easily evaporate in one or two bad months. Melanie felt stuck. An inexpensive solution would improve the efficiency of one or two restaurants but not ten. Melanie had to decide: make a major investment in her business and build her restaurant group, or stay in the kitchen (can you can hear the soundtrack building?).

Scene Four: She now has five restaurants and four times the operating profit. And we are about to upgrade all her point of sale systems next month. More importantly, she has time to do what she loves and a business that generates cash while she sleeps.

The details are determined by the listener. The facts of this story were designed for someone who has a family, was stuck working in the business instead of on the business, and wanted to grow.

Remember, build the script around the person you are meeting with and, like a good movie, the person will put themselves in the story. In about a minute, the customer sees and feels the consequences of not embracing your recommendation and the joy of "winning the kingdom back." To heighten the emotional connection, use imagery to tell the story. Choose a couple of slides that convey the desired emotions, with very few words or numbers. You want them listening to the narrator, not reading. Keep it short. It is better for customers to ask for more than bore them with unwanted details.

As I learned from Clotaire Rapaille, people make emotional decisions and support them with intellectual alibis. Provide the intellectual alibis, but more often, you will need to spend the majority of time on making the emotional connection. Remember the ABC formula, Action=Belief+Care. Most sellers focus on belief. To convert the Unreceptive, place a higher priority on "care."

THIRTEEN

Six Myths About Objections

*When addressing objections, the goal isn't to win a debate but to
validate a customer's concerns and share the truth.*

The most effective response to an objection starts with reframing what you think about the objection in the first place, then how to deal with it. The goal isn't to win a debate. Once an argument begins, influence ends. The goal is to identify and validate their concern and then help them see the truth. When the customer expresses a real objection (versus a false objection explored in chapter 6) it's a positive sign. The customer trusts you enough to engage in a dialogue about a barrier to moving forward.

Unless you've had the opportunity to meet all the players, flawlessly discovered their needs and concerns and can address them when presenting your recommendation, the idea that you will have to address a few of the customer's mental roadblocks before moving forward should be welcomed and embraced. But there are a lot of misguided theories about how to address those roadblocks that can undermine all that you have done to this point to create receptivity. Before we unpack the six most common myths, let's first explore how to ensure decision makers reveal their concerns.

CHECK YOUR SIX

If you are a fan of any war movie or are a pilot yourself, you are likely familiar with the term one pilot uses to signal another pilot to check behind: "Check your six, Maverick. There's a bogey behind you." In military terminology, *twelve o'clock* is straight ahead and *six o'clock* refers to the back of the plane. As you communicate the value of your recommendation, you are essentially leading the customer to a destination, that is, to their "twelve o'clock." Top sellers periodically check their six to make sure the customer is still following, especially when receptivity is low: Are they on track? Are there any concerns? Is what I'm sharing making sense?

The objective of checking your six is twofold: (1) determine relevance and (2) any barriers to purchasing or moving forward. Because of their desire to avoid conflict, most customers would rather avoid communicating bad news. It's just easier to keep their concerns to themselves and avoid conflict. If I had a bad meal at a restaurant and the waiter asked me if I enjoyed the food, I would typically reply, "It was great." Even though secretly I've decided this is my last meal at Tequila and Tacos. This is why we need to assume there are concerns and ask effective questions. If we surface the concern, we have an opportunity to address it.

"Is there anything about ___ that concerns you? If so, can I ask what that is?"

"Which of these do you think best suits your needs?"

"Do you think this would help ____?"

"How does that sound?"

"You seem to be hesitating. Do you mind if I ask you why?"

"How does that compare to your expectations?"

"What else do you need to see or hear before moving to the next step?"

"How will the other team members feel about ____?"

If the customer has none, it's time to advance. If customers are unwilling to voice their hidden concerns, they will most likely surface as you attempt to gain agreement to next steps, especially if that means signing a contract or handing you a credit card. If you uncover a concern, question, or barrier, let's explore a framework for creating the best response by diving into the first myth.

MYTH ONE—OVERCOME AN OBJECTION

"Overcome" positions you against the customer. The word promotes an adversarial mindset. The best way to respond to an objection is with the truth. Your goal is not to overcome, manipulate, or develop an elaborate strategy but to face the concern head-on and simply share what's true. Just as realtors would counsel their mothers about what house to buy, your approach should be the same. We simply need to answer the question "Why is it in their best interest to embrace our recommendation?" This isn't a duel of wits but a partnership in which you stand side by side, look at all their options, and help them pick the one that's best for them.

There is a step before we deliver the truth. As always, we need to validate their point of view.

L.E.A.D. TO WHY

How we respond to the customer when stating a concern or barrier to moving forward is the same four-step response we explored in chapter 9. We need to LEAD—Listen, Empathetically Acknowledge, Drop the Rope.

Let's review based on a common scenario: the customer is concerned about price.

Customer (Susan): That's really expensive, and quite a bit more than our budget.

Seller (Nate): Susan, I may have missed the mark in what I am recommending here. Tell me a bit more about what you mean by "really expensive"? Are you struggling to see the value or is it just outside the funds you have set aside for this project?

Susan: No, I see the value and actually think it's pretty much in line with what we've seen in the market. It's just we hadn't budgeted for phase two. I think we need both phases, but I'm not sure we can afford this right now. Our business is down 20 percent.

Seller: I'm really sorry to hear that. A lot of my clients in your industry are struggling because of ____. If now's not a good time to move forward, of course, I understand. Or we can work together to determine the ROI on the holistic solution you need or pair back to be more in line with your existing budget. Are you trying to determine if it makes sense to allocate more funds to the project?

Susan: Exactly. We want to do it right but may need to go back to the team and expand our budget. We can't have a misstep here. Talk me through how quickly we can reduce our overall cost and how confident I can be that we will see returns on our capital in Q4. Honestly, we have looked at some less expensive options, but I don't think they will ultimately provide what we need.

The seller first "clears their cache" (listens) by realizing that "really expensive" could mean several things: Susan sees the value but doesn't have the funds, or the solution is overpriced, or both. To clarify, the seller asks a question.

As discussed earlier, the brain likes to fill in gaps and make decision based on past experience (other customers in similar industries who chose a cheaper solution). Therefore, here, it is critical to resist the natural response to make assumptions and clarify.

Now that the seller has a clear picture of what the customer means, he demonstrates he understands Susan's point of view and is empathetic to what's happening in the customer's industry (empathetically acknowledges).

Remember, customers are far more likely to embrace our response if we validate their point of view. Once we have complete clarity on the customer's concern, our goal is to validate that perspective and here the magic word *exactly*.

If at this stage you recognized there is much more to learn, you may want to delay your response and take the trip. You will be more effective if you have a complete picture of the customer's business before delivering your recommendation.

Additionally, to further enhance receptivity, the seller clearly demonstrates all options are acceptable: delay, less expensive, or the full solution (drop the rope). By not countering the bad news about the state of the customer's business, Susan starts to feel Nate can be trusted to work together on what is right for her organization.

This is where you may wince a bit at the notion of letting the customer off the hook by stating the willingness to delay the project. Remember, our goal is to demonstrate we are comfortable and willing to explore *all* options. Customers will not use this as a "get out of jail free card." They are not in jail. By acknowledging the power and control that they already possess, your influence grows. Especially when they expect the typical sales response: "Susan, even though it may be expensive, you are going to miss a huge opportunity to . . ." If you pull, they will pull back.

Drop the rope is not a strategy to avoid difficult conversations; it's a strategy to have more productive, difficult conversations.

LEAD to Why—Delivering the Truth

Once you have effectively validated the customer's point of view and are clear about the concern or question, now it's time to communicate why it's in the customer's best interest to embrace your recommendation. In short, the truth.

Why do you charge an additional fee for ____?

Why they need to spend more money on ____?

Why they should add ___ to ____?

Why ____ is more important than ____?

Let's revisit my initial meeting with FedEx detailed in chapter 11. As you may remember, I was faced with one of the toughest objections you can encounter: "I already have what you sell and it's free. Why should I work with you?" Check, please.

From his vantage point, the leader of the inside sales division, Paul, was offered a similar solution from his internal learning organization at no cost. His legitimate concern: "Why should I consider talking to ASLAN?" The underlying message: you are a lot more expensive than free.

It was a legitimate, logical question. He wasn't being combative; he just wanted to know the answer. Watch the move I put on good ole Paul. He didn't even see it coming.

I told him the truth.

No, I didn't respond with the one of the hundreds of techniques found in every book written about sales. I didn't try to overcome his objection. I simply focused on the truth. Why should he invest in an outside firm if he had free access to the same solution?

He shouldn't.

I agreed with his position. No tug-of-war. No argument. No debate. If we offer the same program, the answer was obvious—don't hire ASLAN. Don't hire anyone. Stay the course. That was the truth. And I didn't need a technique to figure this out. I just needed to care about what's best for Paul.

Here's the rest of the truth I shared with Paul. If his free, in-house program doesn't address the eighteen unique competencies required to sell over the phone, then it may fall short. If it was built for field sales, it will likely miss the nuances of addressing the barriers of selling over the phone and have little impact on their inside sales rep's performance.

That was also the truth. A key word is embedded in that dialogue that shifts the conversation from adversarial to collaborative: *if*.

When we are more focused on delivering the truth than winning, you can stand side by side with customers and together determine which path is best for them. Because we were in the early stages of the relationship, I hadn't seen Paul's in-house program. All I knew was the truth about what is required to succeed.

I offered to explore this with Paul, and together we discovered the truth. The free program wasn't in his best interest and we ended up signing a long-term contract.

Does it always work out like this? No.

Sometimes the truth leads the customer in a different direction. But you quickly realize which people you can't help and can be in the best position to influence those you can. Why? Because your position is based on what they should do and not on earning a commission. When your motive is pure and truth is the goal, the right response is fairly easy to see. You don't need Jedi mind tricks to remove objections; you just need a passion for truth.

Whether you face objections as a leader, a sales rep, parent, or even as a spouse, the best response is the truth. Develop your recommendation from the perspective of—what would you do if you were the CEO of their company? Or if you were spending your money? If you're not sure, you don't know the truth, you're left scrambling for a technique or two, and you start to sound like a typical sales rep.

As you think about your response, it is helpful to identify and align your response to the root cause of the barrier. The toughest objections or concerns fall into three categories:

1. There's a legitimate gap. You offer four of the five things on their list.
2. There's a perceived gap. You offer all five, but they are skeptical about the quality or ability to deliver all five.

3. They believe your price is too high. They believe you can deliver all five but they are struggling to see the value.

As we dive into each type and the corresponding strategy, keep in mind these are all based on the belief that the customer *should* buy your solution. If your recommendation is not in the best interest of the customer or they just don't have the resources to invest, the strategies and responses recommended below will most likely backfire.

GAP IN SOLUTION

In objection number one, the customer's decision criteria do not perfectly align with what you offer, but you firmly believe you offer the best solution. Your strategy here is to flank. Change the decision criteria versus promoting a solution that doesn't meet their needs.

For example, based on discovery, your solution is exactly what they need but you are unable to deliver it for sixty days. Unfortunately, they want it now. Your strategy is to validate their point of view and then communicate why it is better to wait sixty days for a better solution.

Your customer will typically have a handful of decision drivers that will determine how they purchase your solution. Rarely will a company be strong in every category. Think through areas where you are weak and the competition is strong and develop your most effective response.

If you offer a solution that is available only in a limited area, you need a response for a customer who needs the solution delivered in all fifty states. If this need disqualifies you from pursuing an opportunity, no response is required. Move on. But if there are situations in which the quality of your solution outweighs your geographic limitations, know why and be prepared to share that truth.

GAP IN PROOF

Often you can meet all the customer's criteria, but because of experience, word on the street, or maybe based on something you inadvertently shared, there is some skepticism. For some reason, they do not believe you, your company, or your product can meet their expectations.

Your strategy is to determine the source of the skepticism and validate reality. The bigger the gap, the more critical an effective word picture, success story, or client referral can be.

Another effective strategy, if possible, is to demo the product or solution.

GAP IN VALUE

In this situation, as in the example above, there is little to no doubt in what you offer, but the customer struggles to grasp the return on investment or payoff needed to substantiate the price. In short, the customer thinks you're too expensive. Now you have only two choices: drop the price or increase the perceived payoff of adopting your solution. The easy path is to acquiesce. The more difficult route is to do the research necessary to convince the customer of the payoff for investing more (we will address this more and how to respond to different kinds of objections later in the book).

MYTH TWO—DON'T TALK ABOUT PRICE TOO EARLY

It's true that establishing the value of your solution is easier once you understand the full picture. But here's the problem. If you resist the price discussion, it is perceived as a negotiation tactic. The battle begins.

"Can you tell me what it costs?" The customer makes a legitimate request.

"Well, I really don't know what it would cost until we spend a bit more time determining what you need," says the well-trained rep.

"Okay, here we go," the customer thinks. "I get that. But I'd just like to know some parameters of what I'm looking at."

"I really want you to see this as an investment," the rep dodges again. "Just quickly tell me about how you will be using our service and we can definitely put together some options that will answer all your questions."

Back and forth you go. Either the customer acquiesces and unwillingly follows your process, damaging receptivity to the ultimate proposal. Or the rep gives in and jeopardizes the opportunity to establish value. Whether the customer is just curious or trying to determine if they can "afford the home before signing up for an hour-long tour," I see the wisdom of answering this question once you have a clear understanding of needs, but you appear manipulative if you are unwilling to provide some parameters of cost. Try this:

To avoid losing a customer early in the process before value can be established, offer the widest range possible from the least expensive to the most comprehensive solution. Deliver the price confidently, much as you would communicate the time.

"Hey, can you please tell me the time?"

"Love to. It's twelve thirty."

It's just a statement of fact. No hesitation that suggests you think you need to apologize for the time of day or you have something to hide. The same is true with price.

"So what do you guys charge for ____?"

"Based on the scope of need, it can range from ____ to ____." Period.

You may be thinking, "But what if I believe I can make the case for investing far more than what the customer initially believes they can afford?" This is a very legitimate question. This is why you want to create the largest variance possible between the lowest and highest investment, a range that keeps a qualified prospect engaged. Regardless, avoiding answering the customer's direct question appears manipulative. That being said, we should sidestep the price trap.

Avoid the Trap

It's not intentionally set by the customer, but it exists, nonetheless. If you attempt to establish the value of your solution without first determining the need for and the impact of your solution, you will most likely fail. Once you answer the decision maker's question about range of costs, the focus shifts to determining the best solution.

We drop the rope by saying, "A less expensive option may be what's best for you or it may make sense for you to invest in a more holistic solution. My recommendation is to spend some time determining what you need, and then I can provide a much more detailed recommendation and proposal."

Or if you quickly realize that the price range is outside their budget, you can drop the rope by saying, "I understand this is outside of what you have budgeted. And I completely understand your hesitation to spend more time discussing your needs. We really may not be a good fit."

Let me pause here and focus on the phrase "may not be a good fit." This is a form of dropping the rope. The more you are willing to go in the seemingly opposite direction than expected, the less pressure the decision maker feels. It also has a counterintuitive effect. As you become more comfortable in communicating the negative, it becomes more likely they will lessen the resistance.

Now that you've dropped the rope, deliver the second half of the message:

"Here's why it still may make sense to dig a bit deeper. A lot of my customers were initially concerned with this size of investment. But for most, after looking at the impact of ____ and seeing how quickly there was a return on their investment, they were able to allocate the necessary funds. If you are comfortable spending a few more minutes talking through your organization's needs, we should be able to clearly determine if it makes sense to continue the process."

Many struggle with dropping the rope, especially early in the process. I get it. It's scary. In many cases you have worked so hard to get to the point at which you're starting to have honest dialogue with the customer and you want to "block the exit." Your emotions and instincts can undermine your end goal. But remember the customer knows you know what your solution costs. Therefore, provide a range, but quickly transition to a discovery conversation to determine value.

MYTH THREE—AVOID TALKING ABOUT THE COMPETITION

A couple of years ago, I decided to evaluate my insurance options. I knew the statistics, and I wanted to make sure that Claire (my wife) could throw a big party if I died. After thirty years of living with me, she deserves a big check. So I reached out to my guy about increasing my policy. After a brief assessment of my needs, he strongly recommended a certain type of policy from the company he represents. It sounded like a good plan, but I wanted to know my options. My thinking was either he had done his homework or I needed to assess all my options.

"Well, that sounds good, but I feel uncomfortable blindly buying the one option presented to me without hearing about all the other policies out there," I told him. "What can you tell me about other policies available? I've heard about policies that . . ." I didn't want my wife to learn about my gap in coverage forty years from now (hopefully). I wanted to figure it out now. I needed to know my agent had done his homework.

It turned out my guy couldn't answer my questions, so the due diligence was my responsibility. I decided to find someone who could unravel the mysterious industry of life insurance. Contrast that with another encounter I had a few years ago at a large trade show.

As I walked the trade-show floor, I was overwhelmed with the options. I wandered up to the first relevant booth and said, "Tell me about your company."

I was shocked by the rep's response. Instead of giving me the typical pitch and avoiding the obvious, the ten other competitors just a
few feet away, the rep put all my options into context for me.

"There are three types of companies in our space," she said.

"Category one focuses on _____ [she gave me a few
sample company names]."

"Category two focuses on _____ [she named a few
more companies]."

"And category three focuses on _____ [a few more
names]."

"We are in category three."

By how she described each of the categories, I was able to quickly
determine where I should spend my time. It was a very other-centered
approach that acknowledged the obvious—there are lots of options
beyond her ten-by-ten booth.

When we act as if no other options exist, the hidden message is
that there is only one choice, the person I'm talking with. And the
customer, who can see all those other "car dealers down the road,"
knows this isn't true. Now you're just another cheesy car salesman.
Does that mean that I bought the rep's solution on the spot? Of course
not. But of all the reps I encountered that day, I remember only one.
And because of the trust and credibility she built, I invested the time
to learn more and was incredibly open to everything she had to say.
Her solution ultimately wasn't a fit, but her approach opened the door
to an honest dialogue.

Here's the punch line: if you can't represent the competition, you
can't be a trusted partner. As a partner, you are required to represent
all the options. Sales reps are often kept outside of the decision-making
process because they sell only what they have. Trusted partners earn
a seat at the table because they are trusted to solve a problem. When
decision makers become more interested in your unique ability to
solve their problem, price often becomes irrelevant.

"But if we don't tell them, maybe they won't know about the competition." That's true . . . if they're buying an airline ticket or renting a car. But a high percentage of customers are going to google it and check out a few options. With a sea of alternatives, you need to be aware and make the complex simple. If you have limited knowledge of the competition, as I did when meeting with FedEx, then offer to spend the time and evaluate the options. If you outwork the competition, they may be your best competitive advantage.

MYTH FOUR—FORCE THE DECISION BEFORE THEY HAVE ALL THE FACTS

Eliminating risk was another reason I was able to overcome the huge price differential with FedEx. Instead of asking them to decide to invest in my solution, I offered a free training program. This reduced the decision from making a huge investment in a relatively unknown solution to observing a free training program. This is an extremely effective strategy to address the value gap—eliminate the risk to determine the value.

Develop steps or offers that allow customers to experience the payoff before you ask them to invest in the unknown. It may slow down the process, but it will increase your wins. "At this point, it's difficult for me to assess if it's in your best interest to pay more. There's more I need to learn about your current solution and your organization. And you know very little about the value of what we offer. Here's what I recommend. Why don't we deliver a pilot program so you can fully assess . . ." For many of you, the customer must see it to believe it.

Maybe it's not feasible for you to offer a pilot program, a free trial, or demo, but think about what you can offer that allows customers to experience the value of your solution. Maybe you can offer a tour, a chance to talk to existing customers, or "lift the hood" to conduct a thorough assessment. When you remove the pressure to buy now, allowing them to determine the value with eyes wide open, they are less defensive and much more likely to honestly assess the true value. Alternatively, if you take the "just trust me approach," it looks like you have something to hide.

When selling your solution, focus on selling the process and not the solution. The question shifts from "How do I get my customer to buy?" to "How can I be sure my customer can assess the value before making a large investment?" Getting a commitment to evaluate a solution is much easier than gaining a commitment to write a check. More on this in the next chapter.

MYTH FIVE—DON'T OFFER THE LESS EXPENSIVE OPTION

Often we are at odds with the customer over the investment required to solve the problem or meet the need. Because of our experience, we're truly convinced the customer *needs* to invest more and the customer is likely to believe we are biased by a potential commission. When faced with this challenge, what's the best strategy? Hammer away on why the more expensive recommendation is in the customer's best interest, ignoring the other options?

Here's the truth: if you offer *all* the investment options, least expensive to the most expensive, you will elevate the desire for the best option.

Let's say you sell an accounting application for which training and support are a sizable portion of the investment. The client is sold on the software but is pushing back on paying for support. Since this is unknown territory for the organization, they're struggling to understand the need.

Based on your assessment, you are convinced buying the support is in the client's best interest. How do you recommend the most expensive option without having your motive questioned?

Consider this response:

I completely understand your hesitation to pay for support when you are unsure, at this point, of what you really need. As you said, this is your first major migration. Here's some questions to consider that will help you determine the support you need:

"Do you have the bandwidth to ensure two to three people can set aside their current roles to champion the implementation?"

"Will they have the necessary time to spend about an hour per employee in the first month of implementation?"

"What are the consequences if your employees experience downtime while learning a new application?"

"Will the internal team have the credibility with the organization to ensure training is embraced?"

The answers to those questions will help you evaluate if your internal team has the bandwidth and expertise to provide the support. If so, there is absolutely no reason to invest in the additional cost in outside training and support. After spending some time with your organization, it appeared that those who could support the migration were a bit overwhelmed and, therefore, you may need additional support. A lot of our customers were surprised at what was required to pull off a successful implementation.

As you know by now, when the pressure is removed, the truth is much more likely to be embraced. Especially in this scenario, where your motive to earn more is no longer the focus. As discussed, the key to this approach is to determine the formula for success. Regardless of who does it or where the resources come from, if you understand and communicate the truth about what needs to occur for customers to reach their desired outcome, they will most likely embrace the best option (A + B + C + D = Desired Outcome).

To bake a cake, you need flour, sugar, milk, eggs, cake pan, oven, and so on. It doesn't matter who provides the sugar or what brand of oven you have. If you want a delicious cake, certain ingredients, along with an oven, are required. I'm obviously overly simplifying, but you get the point. The formula, not the pressure, becomes your best advocate for why the total solution or more expensive product or service is needed.

By willingly exploring all options, whether it's paring down the breadth of services or the least expensive price point on a specific product or service, you send an important message: you don't have anything to hide. Transparency leads to trust. And when trust is established, the decision maker is far more likely to embrace the best option.

MYTH SIX—NEVER GIVE THE CUSTOMER FREE REIN TO DETERMINE THE OUTCOME

A few years ago, one of the largest sales organizations in the world communicated the desire to purchase one of our training programs. The scope was to train tens of thousands of sales professionals annually. That got my attention. If we won, it would be our company's largest and most profitable contract in our history.

We had previously worked with the senior VP of learning to implement a leadership development program, and they were extremely satisfied with the results. Because they were familiar with the receptivity concepts, the SVP believed we had a better approach to helping their sellers prospect for new customers. But as with all large deals, it's never as simple as, "Great, I'll pay your list price of $300 per person. Can you just shoot me the contract?"

Once their decision-making team decided they wanted our program, the contract needed to get through legal, procurement, and ultimately get approved by the president. To use funds earmarked for training by the the end of the year, all this had to occur within a month and a half.

We were working with several major hurdles to getting this deal done:

1. Because of limited funds available, C-level sponsorship was required for an investment of this magnitude. And because of the timing of the request, we couldn't slow down the process and meet with all the players to demonstrate the ROI on tripling learning's budget. If we didn't get it done in a few weeks, available funds would be lost.

2. The company had an allergic reaction to paying a perpetual license for intellectual property. They signed a similar deal a few short years ago, wasting millions of dollars on a program that was quickly shelved. Also, since this was such a large opportunity, potentially doubling the number of people we train in a year, we had no basis for determining a volume discount.

3. If we went through several rounds of back-and-forth price negotiations with procurement, we would run out of time.

Initially, I was at a loss for how to proceed. If I just slapped on the cheapest possible price, making my best offer, it would still be well outside their budget and negotiations would start. There just wasn't the time required and too many layers to follow the typical negotiation process.

I decided not to negotiate. My strategy could be distilled down to three simple words: I trust you. I offered a few data points related to what the market historically pays for content and what they have previously invested to train a smaller audience and then gave the SVP carte blanche to go make the deal happen. I said, "You know what our content is worth, you know all the players, and you know your organization's appetite to invest in this type of solution. You determine what you are willing to invest, and I will accept whatever price you offer. No negotiation. I will agree to whatever you can get approved."

Here was his reaction: "Quite honestly, I'm speechless. Very bold approach. I had already had Susan figuring out how we can make this work on our end. Wow . . . the honesty and trust you are displaying is almost overwhelming . . . I'm blown away. You're placing the utmost confidence in our sense of fair play, though you are correct—we will approach this with the highest integrity. Wow."

This was not a manipulation tactic. This was not a move to get a better result. I did trust the team, so why would I negotiate? Why fight? I dropped the rope, the game ended, and the partnership began. We instantly began working together. They immediately lifted the curtain and revealed the available funds and the probability of getting more. Another unintended outcome that surprised us was they now felt the weight of representing our organization. They suddenly felt responsible for ensuring ASLAN was treated fairly.

The question shifted from "What are you going to charge me?" to "How do we take care of ASLAN?" As a result, the SVP and his team did everything possible to persuade the economic buyers and procurement to increase the investment. They became my advocate. We were friends and team members working together for a common goal. The president signed the deal on Christmas Day.

Did I get a fair market value for my content? Honestly, I'm not sure. But I believe I got the maximum amount of money they could pay for that specific opportunity. Of that much I am confident. If I believed it was a win-lose, they gave me the freedom to walk away, even though I communicated I would honor whatever price they offered. Because I dropped the rope and they were trustworthy, they weren't going to force me to accept a win-lose deal. Yes, I could have rolled the dice, let the existing funds evaporate, and attempted to sell the president on investing more. But that wasn't a risk I was willing to take. I trusted my friend's assessment of the situation.

I am not suggesting you should let every client determine your price. People tend to fall into two categories, givers and takers. Takers are looking for weakness to exploit, and they win when you lose. Givers focus on a win-win. When working with givers, you may want to consider allowing them to determine the outcome.

Most don't have the authority to allow the customer to determine price, but think about what other areas you can allow the customer to determine the outcome. For example, payment terms, try it before you buy it, who's responsible for miscellaneous expenses, cancellation, or even satisfying an unhappy customer (more on that later in this chapter). If you have zero latitude, look for any way that you can demonstrate you trust the customer by dropping the rope.

When the tug-of-war disappears, when you trust the other person and are unwilling to play the game, you are much more likely to receive the best value for your product, service, or solution. Over time, the results will far outweigh those from the adversarial approach. Just the other day, I subleased one of our offices to a good friend in the real estate business. After determining he was interested in the office space, the conversation turned to price. I completely dropped the rope.

"Steve, I trust you. You know more about the prices in the market than I do. You just let me know what's fair, send me a lease, and we're good to go." The translation was, "We aren't going to play the negotiation game. You are solely responsible to represent the interest of both parties. If you would like to take advantage of me, you can."

But here's what I've learned: no one has. The other parties seem suddenly more concerned with getting a fair price than getting the best price. They live up to the trust extended. If you try this approach, will you at some point get screwed? Possibly. But over time, if you build your strategy around trusting the other party, a high percentage will not disappoint.

If you have the authority to attempt this radical, nonnegotiation strategy, consider these four parameters before giving the customer free rein to dictate price:

1. You have a high level of relational equity. Never attempt this approach when dealing with strangers or if you know the person is a taker.
2. A fair market value is easily determined. If the customer can easily see what others are paying for similar services, they are much more willing and likely to represent you equitably.
3. You have a high profit margin. If you can't afford to risk a drop in price, don't attempt this approach.
4. You won't get fired.

Drop the Rope and Let the Unhappy Client Determine the Outcome

It can't be avoided. At some point, there will be a dispute over services rendered. You took the trip to see their point of view and stepped back to consider what's fair, but it's unclear how to respond. Maybe you believe you are in the right, but how do you stand up for what's equitable without damaging the long-term relationship?

They are unhappy in the latest shipment and their request for a refund is clearly unfair.

They are unhappy with the consultant, field engineer, or service tech, and they want a refund or the same service for free.

The service works but not to their satisfaction. They want the more expensive solution for the same cost, when you clearly have lived up to the contract.

We had a situation recently in which the client canceled a project the day before the consultant boarded the plane. The last-minute cancellation cost our firm and the consultant five billable days, not to mention the cost to change flights, and so on. Our contract clearly states the fee for last-minute cancellations. But the client pushed back.

Their perspective was that, given what was happening in the company, the project should never have been scheduled and, as their partner, we should have known that. The message was clear: it was our fault. Our perspective was that the project was scheduled by their point person who felt we should move forward. We were aware of the internal challenges that eventually led to the cancellation, but in our estimation those did not warrant cancellation. The bottom line was, the cancellation was their decision.

To further complicate matters, their point person was no longer with the company. We were faced with the classic he-said-she-said scenario. The VP, stepping in for the missing project lead, felt strongly that the cancellation fee of $7,500 was unwarranted. After an hour-long conversation, everyone had their cards on the table, and we were at an impasse. What's the best response?

Our consultant dropped the rope and let the VP decide. "Jennifer, I totally get your perspective and I can tell you are working hard to understand both sides of the story. Here's what's most important to me: our relationship. So here's what I would ask. You marinate on it for a few days and then let me know what you think is fair. I trust you. If you believe you shouldn't pay a fee, I will cancel the invoice. Just let me know what you want to do and I will happily comply."

She emailed us a few days later and communicated that she believed we should split the difference. Jennifer offered an equitable solution. The relationship was restored, and we covered my costs. Was this a manipulation tactic? Absolutely not. Just the opposite. It was a response based on trust. It was impossible to figure out a resolution that would protect our relationship and equitably represent both parties. By allowing her to make the call, she was free to think through what was fair. And since it was her decision, our relationship couldn't be jeopardized.

If she had decided the cost should be all ours, then we would have accepted that. We made this offer embracing the worst-case scenario. It was a simple decision: Do we want to be right, or do we want a relationship? Easy choice. Since that conversation, that company has spent close to a million dollars with our firm. The VP calls with a need and we respond. We don't haggle about price. She trusts us to offer a fair price, and we trust Jennifer not to leverage her buying power to unfairly cut margin. It's truly a partnership.

Here's what I've learned from working with hundreds of clients over the years: there are clients who will take back their Christmas trees on the twenty-sixth and ask for a refund. But they represent the 2 percent. Don't base your negotiation strategy on the 2 percent. Base it on the 98 percent who desire to do the right thing. They will represent you well and you will enjoy the ultimate payoff: a long-term partnership, trust, and mutual respect. And a receptive listener to every recommendation you make in the future.

PART V

The final stage in selling is the most misunderstood stage in the process. The goal is not to close or sell your solution. Your objective is quite simply to get answers to two questions: Should we continue? If so, how? When you've reached this stage, your role changes. It's no longer about changing beliefs or finding the best solution. It's about facilitating a decision. Here, success is all about alignment. Your mission is to recognize where the other party is in the decision-making process and facilitate a decision about what to do next. Not what you *want* to do but what the customer *should* do. Your role as a trusted partner is to determine the right option and gain an agreement to that option. Every meeting should end with that commitment. Maybe not the commitment you hoped for but a commitment, nonetheless. Once you walk out the door, hang up the phone, or end a Zoom meeting, it may be too late to reengage the customer. Once you leave the castle, the drawbridge may not come back down.

FOURTEEN

An Other-Centered Approach to Advancing the Relationship

Every meeting should end with a commitment to do something. If not, your chances to advance the relationship greatly diminish once you leave the building, a virtual meeting, or hang up the phone.

It was September 6, 2001. I was in New York visiting a client. That night I met John Cerqueira, a fraternity brother of one of our sales reps, who joined us at McSorley's, the oldest bar in New York, for happy hour. John was charismatic, handsome, smart, and witty. I instantly liked him and wanted to hire him. We agreed to stay in touch.

The morning of September 11, 2001, was filled with disbelief, shock, and fear. Then it hit me. John worked on the sixty-eighth floor of tower two. I quickly called Todd, our sales rep, and asked if he had talked to John. No word. We were just one of dozens of messages on his voice mail machine. The most heartbreaking were the ten messages from his mother.

"Please, John. Call me . . ."

What we didn't know was that John was in a life-or-death march down the stairs. We also didn't know that John was about to become one of the celebrated heroes of the 9/11 tragedy.

Instead of rushing out of the building, he decreased his odds of survival by looking for people who needed his help. His search didn't last long, he located a woman in a wheelchair. He, along with his boss, carried her down sixty-eight flights of stairs and made it out the building just minutes before it collapsed. As he gathered his wits, trying not to fixate on the horrific suffering all around him, he began his long walk home in a daze. Suddenly, building two, his building, collapsed.

The world went black. Dust and debris were so thick, he struggled to breathe. "How could I make it out of the building, only to suffocate on the street?" he wondered.

Fortunately for all who loved John, with the help of a firefighter, he was eventually able to breathe. He realized the physical ordeal had ended but knew, like all the other survivors, his life would never be the same. Word spread of John's act of heroism and the media descended. *Good Morning America*, the *Today* show, local stations, reporters from his hometown all wanted to hear his story. He became one of the faces to represent the survivors. He realized he had a story to tell, and through an encouragement of a friend in the publishing business, he began working on a book. Then Oprah's producer called. He was invited to be on the show along with a few other 9/11 heroes. Here's where the story offers some insight for all of us in sales.

He is working on a book. He's having a meeting with Oprah. It was a golden opportunity to ask Oprah if she would be willing to review the book. If she liked it, his book would most likely hit the *New York Times* bestseller list. But that never happened. John did write the book, but very few people heard about it, and very few copies sold. Fast-forward to the present day. John and I have now worked together for twelve years. I've heard him tell this story many times, and here's the wisdom he gained from that experience: once you leave Oprah's show, unless you are already famous, you will never, ever talk to her again.

Unless you leave with an invitation to return.

Here is the parallel truth about the importance of leaving every meeting with a commitment: because of competing priorities and workload, the probability of gaining a commitment to the next step in the sales process greatly diminishes once the first meeting ends. In a recent survey of 483 executives, managers, and professionals, the results of the research highlighted the obvious. People are busy. Sixty percent are connected to their jobs thirteen and a half or more hours a day on weekdays and about five hours on weekend days, for a total of about seventy-two hours. Assuming these people sleep about seven and a half hours a night, that leaves only three hours a day Monday–Friday for them to do everything else (chores, exercise, grocery shop, family time, shower, relax). It also means they spend 62 percent of their waking hours every week connected to work (82 percent on weekdays).

We are all too busy. The point here is that people are so over-whelmed that what appears to be a good idea today will easily get squeezed out by another priority tomorrow. When you're meeting and focused on the related problem or need, that may appear to be the highest priority. The next day, in another meeting, a new challenge, need, or crisis may take its place. Part of it may be due to being so overwhelmed by too much information hitting the windshield that busy decision makers just go where the momentum takes them.

Ever-shifting priorities can also be attributed to how our brains work. Our brains function in one compartment at a time. For example, have you ever been on vacation, getting a little space from work, and see work in a different light? "Why do I get so stressed about ___? I need to rethink my priorities." Why is it that what appeared to be a life-altering crisis on Friday feels a bit trivial on Sunday? We exited the work crisis portion of our brain and moved to the family, friends, or "there's more to life than work" compartment.

Think about the last major confrontation you had with a coworker, spouse, significant other, or close friend. When you were angry, disappointed, or hurt, all the data about the relationship was overwhelmingly negative. You were in the "here's how you've done me wrong" compartment of the brain, and all the positive information to the contrary was a distant memory.

As humans, we just can't keep all the competing priorities front and center at all times. If we could, they would constantly shift as we operate in different zones of our brain. A sales and marketing need might get quickly shelved after a tour of the manufacturing facility. Conversely, efficiency may be the flavor of the month or year until an executive joins a rep on a sales call. The priority instantly shifts to training. What we see determines what we prioritize.

You may be thinking, "If I get a verbal commitment to the next step, couldn't a competing priority bump my meeting off the list?" Of course, but it's much more unlikely if a commitment is made. Multiple studies have been conducted on the power of a commitment, and the results are compelling. Robert Cialdini's research demonstrated that people are much more likely to remain committed to something they verbally agree to. Why? Simply because being consistent, keeping one's word, is an accepted core value. One of our core values as a culture is to "mean what you say and say what you mean."

The goal is not to manipulate but to merely reveal the importance of being intentional about confirming the next step. Procrastination is not your friend. Receptivity to continue the dialogue diminishes, and continues to diminish, as soon as you walk out the door. This is why, if after sharing his story of risking his life to save another human being, John asked Oprah a simple question in the green room: "Hey, would you be open to reviewing my book? It may offer some encouragement to others who have experienced similar trauma." The chances are never greater than that moment for Oprah to say yes. If she does, the likelihood that she would follow through on that commitment is strong.

So now the question becomes: If you should always wrap up the meeting with a commitment, what's the best strategy? Drop the rope and create a fork in the road: agree to work together or purchase, commit to investing more time in evaluating your solution, or agree that they have no interest or need in working together. If you have effectively "checked your six," there should be no surprises here. The goal is to confirm the path forward. Let's briefly explore each option.

Perfect Fit

The customer believes you offer the best solution and they have the budget to move forward. If the opportunity falls in this category, the next step is obvious. Gain an agreement to finalize the financial details, sign the contract, or place the order. The best approach is not to force the customer to say, "I choose you," but to agree on what is required to move forward. Asking the customer to verbally or physical shake hands, like Bud Fox in the movie *Wall Street*, feels contrived and salesy and undermines trust.

Potential Fit

The customer believes your solution is a potential fit, but more information, time, or budget is needed before a final decision can be made. In this scenario, your goal is to gain an agreement to a specific event. To be clear, here's what I mean by commitment. You can send a meeting invite that describes the next event, time, and day it will occur. If you can't send an invite, a commitment hasn't occurred.

"Thanks for the meeting. I'll call you later next week. Have a great weekend," is not an agreement to advance. Until the decision maker verbally commits to a time and day, there is no emotional investment or need to remain consistent with their word. Later in this chapter, we will explore how to develop the next best step.

Not a Fit

Both you and the customer agree that, for the foreseeable future, either the need doesn't exist and/or your solution is not right for the customer or the business.

Here a meeting invite is obviously unnecessary, but commitment is still important. "Why punctuate a bad situation with further rejection?" Fair question.

Remember, your goal is the truth and is not about winning or losing. An honest yes or no is progress. The uncertainty of operating in a fog should be unacceptable. Bringing the decision maker to a fork in the road and agreeing on how to proceed is fair. Neither party wants to waste time on a lose-lose relationship. People generally want to avoid delivering bad news for fear of conflict. Or they would just rather keep things vague, keep their options open. Commitment carries responsibility. Creating a fork in the road brings reality front and center and clarifies the path forward. No judgment, no pressure, just an agreement that pursuing a relationship is fruitless.

Plus, if it appears that you fall into this category, asking for an agreement to that conclusion may reveal the deal isn't dead. Physicians and psychologists know that creating a fork in the road and asking someone if they want to get healthy, change their lives, feel better, and so on can be the catalyst to inspiring someone to change directions. They know that indecision is no decision, and more effort on their part is fruitless.

Additionally, exposing the reality of the situation allows you to maximize your time, and time is the most valuable resource you have. Some studies reveal that because of all the distractions (traveling, administrative responsibilities, meetings) you only have about three to four months per year to hit your number. The top sellers understand that what they choose to spend their time on is the single most contributing factor to their success. Gaining a commitment at the end of every meeting regardless of the outcome, ensures you are investing in only real opportunities. Be unwilling to waste countless hours sending emails, making calls, drafting proposals, or attending meetings about nothing.

Here's what I'm not saying. Pressure the decision maker, prematurely close the deal, or communicate a selfish agenda. Your goal is not to force the decision maker to move in a positive direction but to determine the best course of action and agree on that action. Your motive should always be pure, to serve the customer, and remove the tension by dropping the rope—communicating that all options are acceptable.

If the opportunity falls into the second category, potential fit, you can win or lose the customer by how you attempt to advance the opportunity. The lower the receptivity, the smaller the step.

BABY STEPS

One of the top five most successful bands in history broke up on July 31, 1980. It was a truly sad day because Glenn Frey, Don Henley, and the Eagles practically raised me. Almost daily, as I drove to school in my 1971 Scout, I popped in the eight track tape of *Hotel California*. Thunk. I can still hear the sound of the eight track engaging with the state-of-the art music machine of the late '70s. But my love of the Eagles is not my point here. What's interesting and relevant is how Irving Azoff pulled off the unthinkable.

At the end of recording *The Long Run*, their last album, the band hated one another. The reason doesn't matter, but to illustrate how bad it was, the final straw occurred onstage. F-bombs were dropped, threats were made; it all came out in front of a live audience. The crescendo occurred backstage. The trademark rock star tantrum, smashed guitars, followed by Glenn Frey chasing Don Felder, who narrowly escaped in his limo. They were so done. Henley captured it well in his famous response to the question: "Will the Eagles ever get back together?" He said, "Yeah, when hell freezes over." Subject closed!

What reunited the band in 1994 had nothing to do with the shift of temperatures in Dante's *Inferno* but a brilliant move by the band's trusted manager, Irving Azoff. Before we unpack Irving's strategy, how would you influence a group of extremely wealthy rock stars, who haven't talked in more than a decade, to set their egos aside and reunite? What benefit would you offer?

Money? Maybe, but their bank accounts were full. Plus, the two mainstays of the band had very successful solo careers. Serve the fans?

That might be a good angle but still feels like a tough sell. I'm certain all of the above had been tried by numerous, very persuasive music execs who would benefit greatly by an Eagles reunion.

Irving Azoff took a different approach: he avoided the subject that had been closed for thirteen years and focused on getting the band to just take one, easy baby step. He made a reasonable request: play backup for just one song, to benefit a cause. He didn't ask for a commitment to get the band back together, just for the guys to get together for a short, two-hour recording session for a good cause.

Giant Records agreed to release an Eagles tribute album, *Common Thread: The Songs of the Eagles*. Country's top artist covered the thirteen songs to support Don Henley's charity, The Walden Project. Travis Tritt was planning to shoot a music video of the Eagles' first hit, "Take It Easy." Azoff had an idea and made a few calls. He dropped the rope and invited the guys to the session. They all agreed. Walls came down, relationships began to mend, and the *Hell Freezes Over* reunion tour was hatched two months after the session with Tritt.

Why did Azoff's strategy work? He aligned the event to the emotional state of the Eagles. He changed his agenda from "How can I get them to agree to reunite?" to "How can I get them to agree to be in the same room?" He realized that breaking the process into tiny, acceptable steps was the best shot at getting the band to the ultimate destination. They may be closed to touring but not closed to shooting a video for charity.

To communicate this strategy in a more relevant way: sell your process, not your solution. Develop the steps that will lead the customer to the desired destination, the best solution, and focus on gaining agreement to the next, best step. If you establish a process that helps the customer determine the best solution—not your steps to closing—advancing the opportunity just comes down to alignment. Where they are in the process determines the next step.

Here's the payoff: by developing and recommending an other-centered process, both receptivity and your probability of winning increase. Think steps, not sales. Converting the Unreceptive takes time. Touring your facility may lead to the decision maker experiencing the quality and value of your solution. Offering a free assessment may lead to a presentation to the decision-making team. Watching a documentary on food may lead to signing up for a fitness program.

Here's an example of how you could advance by selling your process in an other-centered way: "Based on what we discussed in this meeting, it sounds like we need to do a bit more work to determine if ____ is needed, and if so, what is the ultimate impact. If you agree, here's what I recommend. Why don't we conduct an assessment in the next two weeks to determine ____? We may determine that you really need to stay with the status quo. Does that sound like a good next step?"

Your role is to lead by identifying and recommending the steps necessary to help the customer evaluate the need for a solution, create an environment in which the truth can easily be expressed about the desired path, and, if working together is potentially beneficial to all parties, communicate an other-centered reason to move to the next step. Closing is not about manipulation, tricks, tips, and slippery dialogue. Maintaining and growing receptivity in this final stage occurs by recognizing where customers are in their journey and recommending the best step to help them evaluate their options. For those of you who hated to close and felt you needed a bath when you heard the words "closing techniques," your role is still to serve, not close. Closing will be a natural by-product of facilitating the customer's journey through the process.

If you get resistance from the customer in the form of a request to speed up the process and skip steps, but you see that this will result in a lose-lose, your goal is to clearly and confidently communicate the consequences of deviating from the process. Your boldness comes from your motive. If you are genuinely concerned that the customer will make a poor decision, articulating why each step is critical shouldn't be difficult if you've thought through the process. If you struggle to respond, assuming you are other-centered, you have more work to do in determining why each step is needed.

What are the consequences to the customer if all the stakeholders don't attend the meeting? If they skip the assessment or demo step, how will that lead to a costly decision? If they want to skip discovery and jump to a presentation, how will this inhibit them from evaluating the solution? Define an other-centered process, identify the steps needed to navigate through the process, and align your recommendation with where they are in the buyer's journey. By following your process, you not only differentiate your solution but separate yourself from the typical rep or manager—the aggressive closer or the one who reactively watches customers flounder as they try to determine how to make the best decision.

RECEPTIVITY DIAGNOSTIC TOOL

What follows is a list of diagnostic questions, organized by each of the five barriers, to help you assess your ability to convert the Unreceptive. This reference tool can also be used to help you prepare for a critical meeting.

When learning something new, it's typical to see performance drop. Therefore, when you are with the customer, be present and do what comes naturally. Avoid the desire to practice new skills or strategies. The time to practice is before the call and after the call. So use these questions to prepare and then review after every meeting. If you do, you will naturally develop and avoid taking a few steps backwards as you apply and test these very counterintuitive approaches to selling.

As you read through the diagnostic questions, you will see a common thread. Did you eliminate pressure, did you make the customer the priority, and do you understand their point of view? If you stay focused on these three essential "P's," more often than not you will convert the Unreceptive.

BARRIER ONE—CHANGING THEIR PERCEPTION OF YOU

To determine if this is the barrier that is keeping you from converting the Unreceptive, did you:

- Pause, prior to the meeting, and reset your compass— deciding to put the customer's needs first?
- Consider all the options and why each one could potentially be in the customer's best interest?
- Demonstrate the expertise to lead the decision maker to the best solution?

BARRIER TWO—OPENING A CLOSED DOOR

If you are struggling to get a meeting, did you:

- Activate the RAS by leading with the customer's point of view (that is, their whiteboard), communicate a disruptive truth, and a proprietary benefit?
- Drop the rope by communicating your solution may not be the best fit for the customer and by asking permission?
- Personalize the message, or does it appear to be a generic marketing message?
- Utilize the framework for an effective introduction (10-30-3) and email?
- When encountering a false objection, have a prepared ADAPT response?

BARRIER THREE—DISCOVERING THE UNFILTERED TRUTH

To determine if you have uncovered the formal and informal decision drivers, did you:

- Primarily focus on taking the trip and validating the customer's point of view? Did you talk less than 20 percent of the time?
- Before the meeting, prepare a discovery roadmap with clearly defined objectives?
- When needed, attach an other-centered purpose or disruptive truth to your questions?
- Communicate, through body language or verbal response, that wrong answers are acceptable and will not lead to conflict?

- LEAD well (Listen, Empathetically Acknowledge, and Drop the Rope) and often hear the magic word *exactly*?

BARRIER FOUR—CHANGING THEIR BELIEFS

To determine if delivering your recommendation is the barrier that is keeping you from converting the Unreceptive, did you:

- Ensure the right people were in the room and you were aware of their formal and informal decision drivers?
- Reframe your role—communicate that your number one priority was to share what others have done to reach the same destination?
- Begin your most important points with "Because you . . ."?
- Consistently offer a new and better way to think about how to solve their problem?
- Clearly create contrast in adopting your solution (either by what you offer or how you implement and support the solution) versus an internal or competitive offering?
- Ensure the customer emotionally experienced the benefit of recommendation by using word pictures or success stories?
- Deliver your message as a peer?
- When faced with pushback, validate their concern and focus on telling the truth and answering their primary question: why it's in their best interest to embrace your recommendation?
- Just need more time? (Sometimes you do everything perfectly and you just need one more ingredient—time.)

BARRIER FIVE—TAKING ACTION

To determine if this is the barrier that is keeping you from converting the Unreceptive, did you:

- Understand where the customer was in the decision-making process and propose the appropriate next step?
- Position the next step as a way to help the customer make the best decision and reduce risk?
- Clearly nail down the next step so that a meeting invite can be sent—agenda, time, and date?

FIFTEEN

Receptivity Is a Way of Life

Receptivity must be more than just a sales strategy. To reach your maximum potential and become a person of influence, adopt an other-centered approach to life.

In February 2009, Steve Kroft, a CBS news correspondent, interviewed the band Coldplay. They had recently released their fourth multiplatinum album in a row, *Viva la Vida* or *Death and All His Friends,* and lead singer Chris Martin was describing his decision-making process for playing certain songs during a concert: "Even if I don't really feel like playing it, those guys have paid their ticket money," he said. "They wanted to see us play 'Yellow,' so we'll play it."

"You wanna give 'em what they came for," Kroft explained.

"And something extra," Chris said, "because when we look from the stage, you can't really see people so much, but you can see the light of the doorway of all the exits. So the way to tell at the beginning of a tour which songs are working, and which ones aren't, is if you see people's silhouettes in the exits, then it means you're probably not playin' the right song, 'cause a lot of people are goin' to get a hot dog, or whatever. So, I know we're doing okay when all the exits are clear. That's my way of judging it. The silhouette factor."

I've heard many artists talk about their work as merely a personal craft: "I can't worry about how people respond to my creative work. I just need to focus on what inspires me," they say. Why, then, does Martin care so much about his audience's reaction to his work?

Whether unconscious or conscious, he has a way of being that goes beyond what he wants. The way he talks about his music and purpose when performing lines up with the most successful and influential people I have met and studied over the past thirty years.

The most successful sellers and leaders are not influential because of what they do but because of who they are. I have discovered they all have a way of living that drives what they do, what they pay attention to, and what they value. Successful people have an operating system not just for work but for all of life. If you want to live a life of influence, learn, as I have, to follow their example. In this book, we began with mindset, demonstrating that an other-centered approach to selling is critical to creating receptivity, then we spent a majority of the book on the "how" of selling and persuasion. In this final chapter, the focus is on "becoming a person of influence," as Stephen Covey put it, by learning four actions that drive other-centered people. As with most things, it starts with a decision.

DECIDE TO SERVE

There's a decision that propels us, that drives us, and ultimately determines our ability to influence. If you go to a travel website to book a trip, there's a box that needs to be filled in first: "What's your destination?" All other decisions hinge on what you put in that box. There's a similar "box" in life that drives how you interact with people and how they respond to you. You have God-given talents and resources at your disposal: time and money. And the decision to make is to answer this question: "What are your talents and resources for?"

You click on the box, and the drop-down menu has only two choices: self or others. Our driving purpose behind everything we do is either to leverage our resources and talents to help others or to serve ourselves. You want ten thousand followers on Twitter. Why? You want to make high six figures. Why? Start a company. Why? Get a promotion. Why?

Anyone who's ever had a quota wants to earn the highest commission possible. We all love winning the deal. I still remember the day

I won my first million-dollar deal: it literally changed the financial landscape of my life forever. Money is fine; there's no shame in wanting any of it. There's no shame even in wanting a lot of influence. All of these things can be good. The question is, what is it all for? Without being too dramatic, this is the biggest decision of your life.

If you have bills pilling up or you're starting a family, you may be thinking, "Survival! Put that in the box." I get it, believe me. We've raised four children while I was a 100 percent commission sales rep. There were times when I literally wasn't sure how we would feed our crew. When we started ASLAN, I had a $2,500 cushion—enough to pay the bills for two weeks. I know what it means to struggle financially. Regardless of your situation, though, we all fill in the blank with something. We all have influence, time, and relationships. Spoken or unspoken, conscious or unconscious, the box gets filled in. Your talents and resources (time and money) can ultimately be leveraged for two primary purposes: to serve yourself or to serve others. It's really that simple.

Why does this matter? I've learned that other-centered people, the ones who click "others," sell more, are more fulfilled, and have richer relationships in life. It's in our best interest to put others first.

If you want to be loved, love.

If you want to be appreciated, appreciate others.

If you want to be significant, chase something bigger than yourself.

If you want to be accepted, reach out to the rejected.

If you want to be the best in sales, serve your customers.

I'm not saying other-centered people don't buy a luxury car or a nice house, that they don't get a massage once in a while, have their nails done, take nice vacations, go to fancy parties, or even buy a boat. I've met some who are extremely wealthy. This decision is about your overriding purpose for existing: your approach to relationships, to work, and to leading. At almost sixty, I've done the research through the decisions I've made and by watching others, and what I can tell you is this: what you and I really want is purpose, not pleasure.

If you are interested in sales and influence, I strongly believe your desire is to live a life centered on others, because that's what sales is really about—serving. We all just need a reminder once in a while that if we don't make this a conscious decision, the box automatically populates. Oh, and there's a catch: you can't and shouldn't serve everyone. Other-centered people choose whom they will serve.

CHOOSE WHOM YOU WILL SERVE

The freedom and confidence to serve comes from choosing well. If we know the investment in others will ultimately lead to fulfillment, a profitable client, and meaningful relationships, serving makes sense. But choosing is never easy.

How do you prioritize the hundred or so waking hours you have in a week? How much time do you invest in family, friends, work, or service? How do you decide which friends are a priority? Which family member should you put first? Which clients or prospects should get more attention? These are tough decisions. Much like determining who gets invited to a wedding, there are always people you care about who don't make the list.

Andy Stanley makes a profound and liberating point in his book *Choosing to Cheat*, in which he says that when it comes to investing in those who are most important to us, cheating is required. In other words, the daily decisions we make every day as to how we spend our time are going to cost something. There are too many people and too little time for us to serve everyone in need. Something or someone is going to get cheated. Just make sure, he warns, that you choose to cheat the things that are not where you ultimately want to invest your time. If we don't make a choice about who or what we will cheat, we'll end up cheating the wrong people.

For most of us, pressure determines our priorities. It's just too easy to respond to the demands of clients, unqualified prospects, and relationships that make the most noise. Think for a minute and ask yourself: Have you ahead of time determined where you will invest your time? What invitations will be accepted, and which ones will you ignore? Other-centered people take the time to choose. Prioritizing your clients and prospects is fairly straightforward (if you need some additional support in building your criteria, a free template is available at www.unreceptivebook.com). The personal relationships, however, are far more difficult. What I have learned is that "cheating" can't be avoided, and if you don't decide whom you will serve, you will most likely serve the wrong people.

SERVE MORE

Think of being other-centered in terms of buying a Christmas gift. You decided to buy gifts for others and made a list of people, and now an investment needs to be made. Intent doesn't result in a present under the tree—other-centered people take action. They don't just serve; they serve more than expected.

Whether serving friends, family, or customers, other-centered people desire to exceed the expectations of those they've chosen to serve. Everyone has an expectation for how they will be treated by others. By going beyond what's expected, we send a powerful message: they matter to us. By serving more, we meet the person's greatest emotional needs: love, acceptance, and worth. Other-centered people care more, learn more, and do more.

Care More

I spent the summer of 1980 riding in an un-air-conditioned truck, delivering five hundred Coca-Cola machines. How did I land this "dream job"? I was dating The Coca-Cola Company president's daughter. I was doing manual labor in ninety-degree heat while he ran a Fortune 500 company and had lunch with the president of the United States. Our worlds couldn't have been further apart, but that's not how he made me feel. He asked about my day and my perceptions of Coke and what it was like to work at the plant. He listened to me. He cared about me, and I loved him. And it wasn't just because I dated his daughter—he treated everyone the same.

This man was a legend at Coke—not only for being one of the most successful leaders there but for how he treated people. He often made surprise visits to the company cafeteria to have lunch with a random employee. He was known for making everyone he met feel like the most important person in the room. Whether he was with Warren Buffett or Susan from accounting, he was sincerely interested in their story, challenges, and life. Don Keough was one of the most influential people I've ever met. People followed him, they listened to him, and his words held tremendous weight. Yes, he was a great leader and an incredible communicator, but how he treated people had far more impact than his talents.

Other-centered sellers don't see their customers as an opportunity. They see people. They feel what the customer is feeling. They lead with love. Genuine love and acceptance is irresistible because it's often unexpected. We are all accustomed to our stories and point of view being ignored with listeners biting their tongue until it's their turn to talk. We are used to customer service reps who do and say the right things but still treat us like customer number 154. If we care more, prospects will share more. They will remember us and buy more.

Learn More

A few years ago, my wife and I were vacationing in Italy and jumped in a taxi. Even though we looked very different than a native Italian, the driver guessed our age. "You're both fifty-one," he said. I was shocked. No one has ever guessed my age. Dumbfounded, I asked, "How did you know that?" He replied in an attractive accent, "I looked at your hands. I can tell anyone's age by looking at their hands. Everyone's hands age the same." He had studied his customers for years and developed an amazingly accurate correlation of hands to age. This illustrates a priceless formula for those of us in sales:

Observation + inspection = intuition.

Regardless of whom we are serving, there are times when we can't fill the gap with questions. Often our intuition is all we can rely on to determine what to say. Instincts are vital when it comes to knowing what analogies to use, what words will resonate, and what level of detail is necessary. We rely on our intuition to determine where to take a client to lunch, when to tell a joke, or whether to provide a friendly hug at the end of a meeting. It helps us determine if the person is angry because of something you said or maybe they're just distracted. Is someone folding their arms because they are closed to the conversation or are they just cold? Developing this level of awareness leads to emotional intelligence that can be obtained only by experience.

Recently, I was in a meeting with a new client, and the VP of sales made a casual remark about the expenses we billed on a previous trip. I immediately remembered that the VP had an unusual path to sales— he rose up through the ranks in the finance department. From years of working with people in similar backgrounds, I have developed a database of information on those who excel at managing money. They typically believe that how you spend money reveals your character, especially if you are spending their money. My "spidey" sense kicked in, and my intuition paid off. We reduced our invoice by a few hundred dollars, and the relationship was restored. Could I have been wrong about the comment? Of course. That's why inspection is critical. The taxi driver also thought we were uberwealthy, because he thought my wife was wearing a $20,000 watch (it was a fake bought in Turkey for a hundred bucks at a place called Genuine Fake Watches). You have to fine-tune this ability with practice.

By capturing thousands of accurate data points, you start to develop a superpower. You sense things others miss. You redirect the conversation when needed. You intuitively know when to change your tone of voice, revamp the presentation, or may even salvage a relationship with a close friend. Other-centered people are not only keen servers; they are keen observers who are intentional about the information they seek. They have a very elaborate filing system.

Imagine an old filing cabinet. Who gets a drawer with their name on it? That's what choosing is about. Serving is about the folders in the drawer. File what the important people in your life value. What will make them feel chosen? What are their unique preferences? How do they like to communicate? What are their personal and professional goals, fears, and greatest joys? What annoys them? What do they love? Who do they love? What dates are important to them? This explains why Joe Higgins, described in chapter 3, was so successful—he learned more. He even knew his clients' shoe sizes.

Think about how you feel when someone gives you a perfect gift, knows how you like your coffee, and senses when there is something troubling you. This perceptiveness meets our greatest emotional needs, and we end up feeling loved and chosen and valued. We have the ability to give this gift to others if we choose.

Do More

In 2007, Frank Blake was hired as the CEO of Home Depot. The company stock was down, sales were behind goal, and the culture had suffered. His daunting task was to revitalize an organization of 2,200 stores and more than 350,000 associates. His leadership philosophy was simple and refreshing: serve the people who serve the customer. He didn't look at the organization in a conventional sense. He believed in the inverted pyramid, in which the customer was at the top and he was at the bottom. He believed that the most significant role in the company was held by those who interacted with customers every day. He was an other-centered leader.

How did Blake demonstrate to the jaded employees that this wasn't just another smooth-talking CEO looking for a seven-figure bonus?

He did more than expected. He put on an apron and lived the life of an associate regularly. Even more compelling, he wrote a hundred personal letters a week to associates to recognize those who had served well. They expected him to visit the store but didn't expect him to work in retail and eat lunch in the back of the building. But that's just what he did. They may have expected him to fire off a few generic emails about serving the customer but not thousands of handwritten notes. By doing more than expected, he made an impact. The culture changed, employee engagement skyrocketed, and performance improved. Under Frank's leadership, the company value increased by 127 percent, net income more than doubled, and Home Depot returned to being the leading retailer in its market.

Regardless of whom they serve, other-centered people make an unexpected investment in others. Whether the investment is money or time, they serve by going beyond the norm, which could be as simple as a phone call or as elaborate as an expensive gift. They find a way to demonstrate more.

To be fully other centered, there is one more action we need to take. The last element of the operating system may be the easiest to grasp but the hardest to adopt, which explains why very few are willing to do the one thing that almost guarantees success—seek feedback.

SEEK FEEDBACK

Cancer is deadly not because we don't have the resistance to fight it but because our bodies don't fight it at all—it goes undetected by the immune system. Like a carbon monoxide leak, if you could smell it, you would fix the problem; but because it's a colorless, odorless gas, it can kill you. Cancer attacks in the same way. If our immune system detected it, it would be destroyed. This is why Duke Cancer Institute's breakthrough research on injecting the polio virus into brain tumors has, in some cases, reversed the cancer. They've figured out a way to trick the body. By injecting a virus that the immune system can detect, the army charges the known enemy. Dead cancer cells are just collateral damage. You hired a pest control company to kill a few pesky rats, but they serendipitously killed a thirty-foot anaconda living in the crawl space.

When it comes to our relationships and careers, there are blind spots that go undetected by our own "immune systems." Psychologists call this "illusory superiority," which is just a fancy term for denial and exists at some level in all of us. The research on the subject, however, is telling. In a study conducted by Cornell University's Psychology Department, 94 percent of professors rated themselves above average, 32 percent of employees of a software company said they performed better than nineteen out of twenty of their colleagues, and out of nearly one million high school seniors, 70 percent stated they had "above average" leadership skills while only 2 percent felt their leadership skills were "below average." On their ability to get along with others, almost all respondents rated themselves as at least average—with 60 percent rating themselves in the top 10 percent of this ability and 25 percent rating themselves in the top 1 percent.

Jack Zenger, the CEO of Zenger Folkman and one of the pioneers in leadership development, once studied 18,336 leaders and 267,116 of their peers and direct reports, comparing perception of the leader to that of their peers. I'll spare you all the data and net it out: those who know us and work with us are twice as accurate as our self-ratings. Benjamin Franklin summed it up well when he said, "There are three things extremely hard: steel, a diamond, and to know one's self."

Other-centered people understand this reality. They know that, because of blind spots and biases, we all struggle to accurately measure our effectiveness. Think of it as a sign above your head that everyone can see but you. Maybe you talk too much or use facial expressions that communicate disapproval when you really are just intently listening. And here's the scary truth: the longer you ignore the sign, the bigger it gets. Imagine that everything you want in life is in a room protected by a locked door. The key that opens the door is humility— to seek and receive information on how you can improve. Everything you need to know to achieve what you want to achieve is available to you if you are willing to ask the difficult questions and unbiasedly assess your own performance.

Consistently other-centered people examine their own motives, observe their own behavior, and solicit input from a trusted source. Inviting others in, as one of my clients recently said, "is when the sh*t gets real!" This is where we begin to see what is on our sign and attack any cancer cells that may be undetected by our immune system.

Seek to Assess Your Motive

Motive is sometimes difficult to discern. I've found the best way to examine your motive is by spotting the clues offered by your behavior. Your behavior, not your intent, always tells the real story.

If you are more interested in talking than listening, your behavior will reveal your motive. If you bristle at constructive feedback, recognizing this resistance will clue you in that your primary motivation is self-preservation and that is more important than improving a defective product—or relationship. If you struggle to drop the rope, these are signs that you need to examine your motive.

That said, being disappointed or desiring a different outcome doesn't reveal a selfish motive. Often, you can't control how you feel, but you can control your response. Paying attention to what you do

and then peeling back the layers to determine why will help you identify if your motive is to serve others or self.

Seek to Assess Your Performance

All athletes that excel at the highest level watch their game films.
Aspiring athletes would be laughed off the field, or kicked off the
team, if they refused to watch and learn from their past performance.
The same holds true for business professionals. To improve, we must
watch our "game films," whether in the moment or afterwards: either
by playing the meeting back in your mind or actually listening to a
recording of the call. Your willingness to review your performances
will separate you from much of your competition, simply because very
few are willing to invite this level of scrutiny into their lives and work.

When we focus on performance, we should not seek only to determine ways we can improve but also how well our recommended solution meets the needs of our client. Our intent to serve the customer
can always be tested by our willingness to ask a question, whether
directly to the customer or to ourselves: "How did I do?" The more
we seek to expose any gaps in how we serve, the more successful we
will be at serving our customers.

Is your self-assessment always off base? Absolutely not, but the
only way to ensure denial hasn't skewed reality is to calibrate your
assessment with the feedback of others. Maybe you did lose five
pounds, and the scale is just wrong. The only way to determine the
truth is to step on a few other scales and calibrate. If you are unwilling
to test your reality, this is your first clue that a cancer may be growing.

Seek Feedback from Others

Now we are going where few have gone before, but if you are willing to
risk this level of exposure, you will see the most significant impact on
your ability to drive receptivity and overall success as a human being.

Other-centered people ask others to help them see their blind spots. How does it work? You simply invite a few trusted friends and associates, those who have observed enough of your interactions, to help you discover the unvarnished truth about you. At first, you will have to overcome a bit of skepticism. Most will assume the meeting is more about getting a compliment than actual improvement, so address this head-on and ensure the other party is clear on your intent. It's okay to acknowledge that positive feedback is always appreciated—it's good to reinforce what you do well—but your desire is to expose your blind spots. Say something like, "I know I am not perfect and I can always get better, so, as a trusted friend, I really would appreciate your input."

Second, this must be a planned event. Creating an environment where honesty flows requires some planning and time and a place to meet. You don't want to casually ask over lunch, "So what do I need to work on? What are my blind spots?" You both need time to prepare. They need to think through a few preplanned questions, and you need time to emotionally prepare to receive the information. Here are a few questions to get you started:

- What have you observed in my interaction with customers/ prospects that inhibits me from focusing on their needs or tuning in to what is most important to them?
- Do I adjust my approach to each customer, or do I approach most customers with the same questions, presentation, relating style, and so on?
- How well do I listen to others? Do I tend to tune out when other people start talking? Do I talk too much? Do I seem genuinely interested in and care about those I work with?
- What are the top three things (skills or strategies) that are inhibiting my performance?
- What do you see as a unique talent that I could leverage more effectively?
- What are you afraid to tell me for fear it might hurt my feelings?

- Why do you hate me so much? (That was a joke. Don't ask that question.)

Remember, their instinct will be to answer the questions with a positive response. Initially, they will not trust the sincerity of your request or that this conversation will end well. So, like a great seller, continually remind them of your motive to improve. And remember, the wisest response to feedback, whether good or bad, and regardless of who delivers it, is a singular question you ask yourself: "Is it true?" Don't assess how it's delivered, who delivers it, or why the message was delivered. Use it for your good. If untrue, discard it. As I used to tell my kids, "If one person tells you you're a horse, ignore them. If five people tell you you're a horse, buy a saddle."

As you consider this, you may be thinking, "There is no way in hell I'm handing someone a knife and inviting them to stab away!" I get it. Facing the truth about ourselves is painful, but here's what I've learned: avoiding pain leads to more pain. Denial is like the mother of the contestant on *American Idol* who tells her tone-deaf daughter that the four Grammy-winning judges are wrong. By rejecting the wisdom of the judges, the singer lessens the sting but misses her chances for improvement. If we embrace the need for feedback as a tool to achieve our goals, the pain can be diminished and even eliminated. The key to lessening the sting is to be the initiator, to seek it out. Asking a friend and finding out you have less than fresh breath is far less painful than finding out after the party that you needed a mint. I always try to remember that the sign above my head is visible to everyone who knows me. Just because I can't see it doesn't change reality.

If adopting an other-centered operating system is a new thought for you, test it. For a month, decide to put others first. Spend some time determining whom you will serve, both personally and professionally. When you have the opportunity, serve more and end the month with a sober conversation with a trusted friend. Then analyze how this new operating system affects your relationships and ability to influence (a free other-centered assessment is available at www.unreceptivebook.com). In twenty-five years of sharing what I've learned about being other centered, I've never had anyone tell me that they wished they hadn't served so well.

What they tell me is that dropping the rope, taking the trip, and being other centered not only made them a better seller, it made them a better spouse, parent, friend, and neighbor. They tell me that they are more fulfilled when they serve.

The successful motivational speaker Zig Ziglar once wanted to communicate a very important idea: life is about faith and serving others. If you trade the quick fix, the temporary high of chasing money or pleasure for your own consumption, for something more lasting and more meaningful, it is worth it. Trade the pursuit of pleasure for peace and purpose. He wanted his audience to know we are more fulfilled when we serve.

But how can you convey this message to an audience when almost everything we see and read tells a different story?

He brought one of those old water pumps onstage. You know, the kind you see on an old farm, used to hand pump water out of a well in the late 1800s. Priming the pump and creating the suction needed to get the water moving required pouring a cup of water in the priming port. Zig asked the audience to close their eyes and imagine they had been walking through the blazing-hot desert for days, so thirsty they would suck water out of mud. Then he asked them to imagine they see the pump, along with a jar of fresh water and a note, which reads:

"Drink this water and it will be gone. You'll save your life . . . for a while. But if you pour this water into the pump and prime it . . . then pump really hard for a long, long time, you'll have more water than you can imagine . . . enough to satisfy yourself and everyone with you. And you'll have plenty to refill the jar for those who'll come after you."

Taking this precious water that you needed so badly and pouring it into what could be a black hole seems like insanity. Who would do that? But if you do, if you keep pumping with no evidence of progress, there will be a reward. You will trade one cup for a permanent supply of refreshing and life-giving water. It's everything you wanted and needed, and there's plenty for those who will come after you. You will trade the temporary satisfaction for long-term fulfillment. That's what it means to be other centered, and that's what receptivity is all about.

WHAT THIS IS ALL ABOUT

The first fourteen chapters were about what we need to do before and during the meeting to convert the Unreceptive. This last chapter, however, is about how the most influential people live and operate every day. It bears repeating that who you are and how you live have more impact on your ability to convert the Unreceptive than what you do in the moment.

Most of the world's top performers understand this intuitively, that what we do when we are preparing for what's to come is where the real growth happens. For the athlete, there's game day . . . and then there's what you do when you are not playing the game. What you do to prepare to play is far more important than what happens when you get on the field. For the stage actor, there are the hundreds of rehearsals leading up to opening night that make that one performance excellent. And for a musician, what you do when you are not performing determines what will happen during the concert. Before most people knew his name, John Mayer spent years alone in a room practicing. As John Lennon once said, "Life is what happens to you while you're busy making other plans."

If you want to be a person of influence, you must focus as much on how you live as you do on how you work. Yes, to develop the advanced skills required to influence the most difficult category of customer, we need to prepare for the call and ask ourselves the tough questions. This is our work. We need to learn what it takes to get a meeting, validate the customer's point of view, and reframe how we craft and deliver a message. But outside of the meeting is where we really hone these skills and learn to master them. It's where we move from amateur to pro.

The most influential and fulfilled people in the world live differently; they are other centered. And almost everyone they meet is receptive to what they have to say. They are open to what these special people have to contribute, because their life clearly isn't just about them, and this makes them trustworthy. May it be the same with you.

INDEX

ABOUT THE AUTHOR

Tom Stanfill is CEO and cofounder of ASLAN Training, a global sales enablement company appearing nine consecutive years in the *SellingPower Top 20*. Since 1996, ASLAN has worked with many Fortune 500 companies, training more than one hundred thousand sellers and leaders in more than thirty-five countries. To learn more, visit ASLANTraining.com.

Tom lives in Atlanta with his wife, Claire. They have three sons and one daughter. This is his first book.